QUEEN OF THE MUSIC HALLS

Uni   ®

MARIE LLOYD

QUEEN OF
THE MUSIC HALL

Being the dramatized story of

MARIE LLOYD

By

W. MACQUEEN-POPE

OLDBOURNE

PRINTED AND BOUND IN GREAT BRITAIN
BY JARROLD AND SONS LIMITED, NORWICH

CONTENTS

Uni   t ®

I

MUSIC HALL!

THIS is the story of an Immortal. No class or stratum of Society has the monopoly of those remarkable individuals. They are just as likely to be found in the Whitechapel Road as in some cloistered Oxford College, in some suburban villa as in a mansion matured by the centuries—in a grammar or secondary school as in a great public school of hallowed tradition. It is the individual and not the surroundings which make them; they are born to immortality and achieve it, no matter against what odds. Art, Literature, Science, Medicine, Politics, Philanthropy, Philosophy, the Fighting Services, the Drama, the Stage, Commerce, Engineering—every profession and calling has them; and so had even a peculiar branch of public entertainment which has now become extinct in its genuine form because it served a particular era of Life; and that particular entertainment form was the Music Hall.

Music Hall existed for barely one hundred years but in its day, so vital and so strong was it, that it raised its immortals. Few in number, it is true, but they were great in achievement, few but very select, and in their own line, very great too. None of them was greater or better beloved than a woman known to the world as Marie Lloyd.

In other countries Marie Lloyd would have been

far more greatly honoured than in her own. France has its regular table of immortals, but here they exist only in public memory and by being handed down by word of mouth. Some will cling to their immortality by means of graves in Westminster Abbey or St. Paul's Cathedral; others lie in cemeteries cheek by jowl with the people they served and who made them. So it was with Marie Lloyd. There is no monument to her save one of remembrance, and as the generations go by, life changes so quickly that even that may fade, although it is probable that her name will be perpetuated by means of some of her songs, which are now a part of the folk-songs of this country, and, most unfortunately by a reputation, or sub-reputation, which she did not deserve. But she is as worthy of remembrance as any of the immortals whom the ordinary man in the street regards as highbrow. For she was the epitome of the womanhood of her class and day, and of the particular phase of the English way of life which she lit with her genius. So perhaps, this little book may help to serve a purpose and kindle a flame in the memory of a generation which knew her not.

Marie was so typical of that great, virile surge of British life which ruled the world in the days of Queen Victoria and the Edwardian Age, that it followed she was absolutely typical of the entertainment form which she adorned like a lustrous diamond. We called it the Music Hall and to get her into true perspective it is necessary to understand Music Hall, as it was then.

There is no such thing as real Music Hall today.

There is something called Variety, which is very different. Variety often defeats itself by contradicting its own name in its own achievement, but Music Hall was Variety in the true sense of the word. It gave something of everything to every kind of taste. It was, quite simply, entertainment of the people for the people by the people. It came out of the inns and the public houses, it ascended to Empires, Coliseums and Palaces, and it catered for people individually and collectively by means of individualists. Its performers were the great individualists of the entertainment world. It was when there came a change of public taste, and that happens at regularly recurring periods, that its individualists sank their individuality in the team work of revue and Music Hall began to die. The talking pictures completed its downfall and it took refuge, once again, in the public houses from which it had sprung. But the public houses were now smart hotels and music hall called itself cabaret—a foreign name ill suited to such a peculiarly British institution.

Music Hall first arose to supply the wants of the industrious working class who had little or no entertainment provided for them. There was the theatre, but that was expensive and did not really give them what they wanted. And what they wanted was homeliness, companionship, friendliness and a feeling of participation, an intimate touch in which they could feel a personal note. When the Victorian Age began to give employment through the surging upgrade of industry, a man called Charles Morton, who had been a waiter, a bookmaker, and a licensed victualler, hit upon the very method of giving people what they wanted. In the Canterbury Arms in the Westminster Bridge Road, then better known as the Lambeth Marsh, a tavern with a very old licence which had occupied its site for centuries and which was steeped in hospitality, he opened a singing-room in which artisans, tradesmen, shopkeepers and the like could find entertainment, and to which they could bring their womenfolk. There was no charge; he took his profits out of the drinks consumed, but he saw to it that the entertainment was the best he could provide. The public liked it, liked it so much that he built on a piece of spare ground adjoining, the first real Music Hall, the Surrey Music Hall—and in 1854 Music Hall was really born. The accent was largely on music and singing and melody was the staple fare. There was also the variety which Morton had observed was pleasing in the supper rooms and the clubs, prices for which were beyond the purses of the people for whom he catered. Music Hall was aimed at ordinary working men and it found its target. It gave them good music—the music of Gounod's *Faust* was first heard in London at the Canterbury Music Hall; it gave them the skilled artistry of the acrobat and tumbler, the magician, the instrumentalist, and it gave them the comedians and comediennes, presenting them all in a manner which was direct and free from anything concerned with art, which in this country was then highly suspect.

Music Hall gave people exactly what they wanted. It was an enormous success. The audience sat at tables and ate and drank as the performance went on.

It appealed to the people in language and terms which they understood. It was completely down to earth. Its comedians sang to the audience about their everyday life, about mother-in-law, the lodger, the woman next door, beer, the public house, the seaside holiday, the landlord, the unpaid rent and the brokers' men, about food and drink—and also about that ever present difficulty to which it referred in its own language of rhyming slang as 'The Trouble and Strife'. But it was, of course, always implied that one's own wife was different and excluded from this category. It turned the little worries of existence into things of fun; it made people laugh at what had been worrying them, to see the funny side of life and thus it cheered them up. It was vulgar of course, but it was vulgar in the best and truest sense of the word. It was as vulgar and as British as Hampstead Heath on a Bank Holiday and there is no great harm in that! And per contra, it was highly moral. It glorified true love, it denounced fickleness and marital infidelity. It placed happy married life on a pinnacle; *My Old Dutch* remains to prove it.

It sang of duty and bravery, and it purveyed a high sense of patriotism when patriotism was something of which nobody was ashamed. It waved the Union Jack to audiences which responded fervently. People then had pride in their flag and believed in their Empire, even if they knew very little about it. It took little account of foreigners—who were figures of fun. It was quite certain that one Briton was equal to any six aliens—and its supporters believed it, too. It told the people for whom it catered that it had an invincible Navy, and that its Army, although small in size, had the habit of going a damned long way. It was intensely loyal to the Crown and to the country. It had a certain spiciness and naughtiness which was never dirty or leering with salacity, but which had the honest bawdiness of Shakespeare. And so, giving the people exactly what they wanted it was a success. Very soon, people of all ranks and classes crossed the bridge of London to the Surrey side and to the Surrey Music Hall. And, of course, Music Hall began to spread and spread. It went like wildfire, urged on and driven by popular taste. Within twenty years of its beginning, it was one of the two great forms of public entertainment, challenging the theatre for supremacy, and, in many parts, far more popular. The theatre, always conservative and restrictive, tried to fight it by means of repression, by attempting to stop the miniature dramas, called sketches, which Music Hall made part of its bills. But the Halls won. They won because they had a vast section of the public solidly behind them and because they could offer so much.

Here, in the Music Halls, more than anywhere else, was the true expression of the age of beef and beer, of full-blooded success and supremacy over the world, of full-hearted and full-throated enjoyment, of a way of life which was not complex, which had never heard of inhibitions or psychiatrists, and which did not deal in understatement. The world was a place of high colours, and Music Hall reflected that. Sentiment had its place. But it was good, honest sentiment and not mawkish sentimentality. Gloom and depression had no place in it. The sad songs which nowadays come across the Atlantic in shoals would have found no echo in those hearts which found joy in Music Hall. Music Hall was a holiday, a place mainly for joy and laughter and for a very high expression of the art of entertainment. Let there be a tear now and again, but let that tear be only the necessary shadow to heighten the brightness.

Those audiences which flocked to Music Hall went there for a holiday, and got it. They got a mixed bag of talent which was most remarkable. They got an atmosphere and a friendliness which engulfed them as soon as they entered its doors. They became part of a crowd of people who were happy, and what troubles they might personally have soon fell away. Music Hall made every night a Saturday night. One of the reasons for the extinction of Music Hall is that the audience for which it catered is no longer there. People have changed, outwardly, if not inwardly, and life has changed around them. Music Hall, like the theatre, had to reflect life. Music Hall audiences were part of the show, they were the pivot on which it turned. And also, to get the atmosphere they created, which was also an integral part of Music Hall, it was necessary to have them all together in one place where the strange human electricity they generated, infected and energized the individualists who appeared on its stage. That audience, although it came to be entertained, was, nevertheless, highly critical. It would stand no nonsense. It knew what it liked and what it did not like. It made no secret of its feelings. It would condemn in unmistakable terms, but it would applaud and praise in terms equally unmistakable. It was intensely loyal to its favourites. Once it took a performer to its heart, only that performer could bring about his or her undoing, by misbehaviour or by letting its audience down. That seldom happened.

The audience was not saturated by entertainment. It did not sit at home in the dark or semi-dark and twiddle a knob and stare at a screen. It went out from its homes, it got among friends, into a place charged with anticipation and happiness. It could smoke, it could have its drink, and it could let itself go. It was having 'an evening out'—away from the atmosphere of its home, so often fraught with care and anxieties. It paid very little for its entertainment, but it got tremendous value. For the Music Hall knew that only the best was good enough, and it gave immense value for money. You could see a bill of stars for a shilling, the like of which could never be assembled today. And those stars were all different. The audiences loved them, and often refused to let them do anything new. They liked the old acts, the old songs—because they did not see them so very often—maybe once or twice a year. Some acts never changed their material in forty years. But that is not to say there was no variety. There was. Especially in the songs. These great artistes were perpetually getting new songs. Songs which were written for them to suit their art. And for the greater part, those songs linger on in the memory and have become folk-songs of our race.

Those artistes who made Music Hall were, in the main, people of quite consummate art. They understood audience control, they understood human mentality and they understood 'attack'. They understood, above all else, how to exploit their own gifts, their own individuality. There might be many who sang the same type of songs, but there was always some subtle difference—a difference of personality and individuality. They had force, and they had clarity of diction. They made no pretence of refinement or preciosity. They sang in their own natural voices and their own natural accents. They did not assume an accent which belonged to a foreign country. If they were Cockney, what of it? If they were North-country, so much the better. If they were Scottish, well, that was their strength and their appeal. And one and all, they were British to the backbone. There were amongst them many who were not of British birth, but they became as British as the next man because they became part of Music Hall. They were stars because of that; not because of their nationality. The time had not come when, in Music Hall, the way of other nations was considered better than our own. That might be so in other branches of Art, but not in Music Hall. Music Hall, too, was a place of great efficiency—not only on the part of the performers, but on the part of the mechanics of the place. Music Hall had a time-table as rigid as that which exists in the studios of the B.B.C.—but rather differently administered. An 'act' knew exactly at what time it had to take the stage, it knew exactly how much time it had thereon, and it knew that it must not be late and it must not overrun.

Also, as time went on, the men and women of Music Hall had time-tables of their own—they would appear at three or four halls on the same evening and they had to keep time. They did, too, by their own efforts, and mostly by horse-drawn transport. They had not the stagnation of traffic brought about by the internal combustion engine, which defeats its own speed by congestion—by hold-ups on Tubes on account of failure of mechanism or absence of staff. And, if a delay was caused, as some-times it was, by a tremendous success which 'stopped the show' or by an unforeseen accident—well, the Music Hall bill, being human, could cope with that and alter its running order—which is impossible with the mechanical entertainment provided today. Only world-shaking events can alter a broadcast or tele-vision programme, but the Music Hall dealt with all mishaps by human means because it dealt with humanity. Those people of Music Hall were a race apart. They never sought publicity. They kept them-selves to themselves. They became, therefore, inhabi-tants of the land of illusion, only seen behind the frontiers of their country, which were the footlights, and there they were seen to their greatest advantage. One paid to see them, therefore they had value. They did not mix with the ordinary world; you seldom, if ever, saw them at public functions or at smart, popular rendezvous or restaurants. They had places in which they congregated. They wanted their public to love them, and their public did just that. But they did not want to cheapen themselves by familiarity. And they never did. They would not have submitted to being called by their Christian names before millions of people by a young lady or gentleman whom they had never seen before. They did not crave a place in gossip columns or in the general news. Their best publicity was themselves and what they could do. By and large, the West End of London meant little to them. It was just a 'date' to be 'worked'. Manchester was as good as Mayfair, Glasgow as Golders Green.

Between the people of Music Hall and the people of the theatre there was a subtle difference which was illuminating. The people of the Halls called themselves 'performers'—and how right they were. And whereas the actors and actresses 'played' at a place or a theatre—the performers 'worked a date'. It put the whole thing in a nutshell. They lived in little colonies of their own—in Kennington, in Brixton, in Canonbury and Stoke Newington, in Islington, and later in Golders Green and Streatham. They were, by and large, as decent, respectable, and law-abiding set of people as any in the land. There were black sheep amongst them, but so there are in any section of the community. They were considered Bohemian, and so they were, inasmuch as their manners and customs did not conform to the conventionalized respectability which surrounded them. But they were not immoral, they were not lewd, and they were not loose-living. They always faced intense competition.

They had only themselves on which to rely, and that kept them on their toes. They had a standard to maintain when they achieved success, and they never failed to maintain it. They lived for their work and they must never let their masters down. Although they were individualists, they knew that the public were their masters. They always put their work, the show, and their public first. If they were out of the bill, it was by something over which they had no control. If they could stand up and give their show, they did it. But that public looked upon them as their friends and treasured them. They called them by their Christian names amongst themselves, and they flocked to see and applaud them. Those who reached that coveted position known as 'Top of the Bill' did so by sheer talent. And they had to hold it by the same means. They had no help, no elaborate scenery or stage-bands, no background of glamorous girls. They had no shouting announcements and appeals to 'give the little girl a big hand'. They were—themselves. If they slipped, they slipped into oblivion—there were no sidelines—no small parts as in the theatre. And it was oblivion they feared. There were those amongst them who, when they feared that defeat was upon them, took their own lives . . . that was how they felt about it. All the announcement they got was their name on the bill and their 'number' in 'the frame'—that is, the number of their act on the programme in lights in the frames which were on both sides of the proscenium to let the audience know what came next. But that was enough. There were some names that caused little effect when their numbers went up, and there were plenty which caused a buzz of excited anticipation. And there were a few—fifty or so, which got preliminary applause. But there were some which made an audience become all eyes and ears, sit forward, applaud, and even cheer when those cards were changed or when those lights flickered. Those were the names of the immortals— and one of those which caused the greatest stir, the biggest applause—the greatest eagerness and the combined 'Ah-h-h-h!' or 'Oh-h-h-h!' of expectant pleasure was the number which signified a woman who was in herself all those things which combined to make Music Hall the power it was—and that name was Marie Lloyd.

Marie had no big adjectives against her simple name on the programme; there was no declaration that this was the greatest artiste in the world; that she was sensational, supreme, magnetic, terrific, the idol of millions, the zenith of sex appeal, the sweetheart of the world. She billed herself as 'Marie Lloyd— Comedienne' or 'Soubrette'. It was enough. Only towards the end 'Queen of Comedy' was added.

For years she reigned supreme—not only in this country, but all over the English-speaking world. She was one of the few Music Hall artistes who really conquered America. Her name was a household word. She was 'Marie' to everyone and millions whom she had never seen, except through the smoky haze of the Music Hall footlights. But those who had seen her time and again, loved her. For although she was aloof from them by virtue of her calling, she was also their dearest friend. They felt they knew her intimately.

This she achieved because she was a woman in every sense of the word—she was the whole world of woman in her own small person. She was the woman of Mayfair and the Mile End Road, of Regent Street and Ratcliffe Highway, of the saloon bar or the jug and bottle department. Also, she was one of the audience, she understood them and they understood her. She had songs which appealed to them in every way; and she had that strange thing called glamour. It was not the artificial glamour of cosmetics, but the real thing. She had an audience held captive even before she stepped on the stage. And, above all, she had radiance, which shone more brightly than all the lights of Piccadilly Circus or Broadway. Marie Lloyd was radiance and radiance was Marie Lloyd. And that radiance made her an immortal.

II

THE BEGINNING

THE story of Marie Lloyd begins in a place called Hoxton, a suburb in the north-east of London which had once held good houses and wealthy people, but had decayed and already gone down the social scale by the time that one of its most exalted natives drew first breath there. Like so many districts, it had fallen from open country to select residences, then to a lesser degree of social status, and then to commerce. London is ringed with such bands of social descent, and the outward movement still goes on. It had become a place of factories and of working people. It was not the sort of district in which one would look for genius or brilliance, yet it produced something of that kind. Strangely enough, it produced two people who, in their time, did more for the brightness of the nights of London than anyone else before or since, a boy and a girl. The boy was John Hollingshead, who built, founded, and indeed created the Gaiety Theatre and all that it stood for; and the girl was Matilda Alice Victoria Wood, daughter of John Wood and Matilda his wife (*née* Archer), whom the world was to know and love as Marie Lloyd.

There was something which was, perhaps, prophetic in the little Hoxton house into which that tiny baby girl was born, on February 12th, 1870, for the

name then of the street where it stood was Peerless
Street. Into Peerless Street someone peerless was
born.

The parents were respectable, hard-working people.
The father made artificial flowers, working for an
Italian merchant who dealt in them. He was a first-
class workman who had imagination, for he had ideas
which made the flowers he manufactured better than
those made by others. He constantly made improve-
ments and added touches which brought the artificial
nearer to nature. He had, it seems, the creative spirit,
which his little daughter inherited. But he was an
easy-going man with little push or initiative in his
own affairs, contented with his lot and not on the
look-out for advancement. Probably he had the
artistic temperament. The mother was far more
forceful. She knew her husband was worth more than
he earned and was always trying to spur him on to
make a stand for himself. She, too, helped her
husband to make the artificial flowers, and had great
aptitude, although she took the craft up with no
training. There was nothing aristocratic in the background of either. His forebears had been country
folk, cutting osiers and willows and making them
into bonnets. Her parents had been bootmakers. But
in the mother's family there was a slight theatrical
strain—there was a dancer and a comedienne.

They earned between them a little over two pounds
a week when their first baby was born, yet they lived
in comfort, and saved. Mrs. Wood was an accom-
plished housewife, a woman who took pride in her
home; she kept the tiny place absolutely spotless and

shining, a habit which that first child, Matilda Alice Victoria, was to inherit. The nomenclature of the little fair-haired, blue-eyed, and remarkably vigorous and healthy baby speaks for itself. Matilda was the name of its mother; Alice is not so clear, probably a relative on the father's side; but Victoria—well, the great Queen was thus, in a sense, the godmother of the Queen of the Halls, although she never knew it: and probably would not have liked it had she done so.

The baby was called Tilly—but as soon as she was able to do anything about it herself, she showed the force which was within her and rechristened herself. She called herself Marie, a name she herself liked—pronounced Mahry—with no ridiculous foreign falal at all. As was the manner of those days, the family increased rapidly, and soon Tilly was joined by Johnnie, Alice, and Grace. And, except for Johnnie, they were little rosebuds of fairness and high colour. The Woods moved to larger premises. They had to, and even with her family cares upon her, the mother worked on at her flowers, and at fancy-costume work which she did at home for a factory near by. She had to stay at home because of the children. She was always trying to get her husband to make a stand and get more money from his parsimonious Italian employer, but Wood never had the pluck or the drive to stand up for himself. Children continued to come to the little Hoxton home with steady regularity. Altogether there were to be eleven of them, quite a respectable number, even for Victorian days. There were always new mouths to feed; there was always need of money. The arrival of those children, those helpless little babies which, for a time, a very short time, would lessen the income of the family by putting the mother out of the weekly increase in the pay packet, had a result. The small Tilly showed her force and her individuality. This pretty, golden-haired speck began to 'mother' the little ones, to take charge and to take responsibility. To understand what had to be done about a house, to appreciate what a woman's work could be—and what a wife's work always is. And although she did what she could, she made up her mind that the man who went out to work had the better job. It was, perhaps, the first lesson which shaped her destiny. There was something else, too. If one is to get one's living in the world of entertainment, if one's destiny is the stage, signs and portents show at an early age. They do not always work out, for many children have stage ability in their early days which vanishes when the self-consciousness of approaching adolescence comes upon them. But it is usually pretty easy to tell those who have the divine madness in them—for that strange thing called personality dominates them. The tiny Tilly of Hoxton had shown that she had personality almost from birth, and it grew stronger. She could express herself—and she had force. It would seem, although details are lacking, that she learnt a little jig from her Aunt Louisa, the dancer, who took her to some hall, nobody knows where, and let her dance it. People were delighted and deluged coppers upon her. Throwing coppers could mean displeasure, but in this case it was pleasure, which the small child, about four years old, brought home in triumph. She would take a little basket with her, when she was allowed to accompany her aunt on these jaunts, and bring it home full. But quite early on, she experienced the setbacks which all artistes must endure. There came a night when nobody threw any pennies, and she was disgusted. She never danced that way again. She was a most determined young person.

But she soon showed that she was an individualist. She did not like any form of repression or discipline. She did not like school. But she could, and did, compel obedience in others, and she ruled her small brothers and sisters with a rod of iron. And she insisted that they should be very clean and saw to it that they were by washing them herself. That was her mother in her, and all her life she herself, Marie Lloyd, was the very essence of personal cleanliness. It was part of her radiance. That radiance was about her as a child. It showed in her fresh, rosy cheeks, her golden floss-like hair and her shining teeth, which protruded slightly beyond her upper lip as if to show the world how white and regular they were.

To augment the family budget, upon which increasing demands were constantly made, John Wood worked overtime. By day he made his flowers —and at night he was a waiter. He waited, not at public dinners or in restaurants, but at places of public entertainment, where in those days drinks were served in the auditorium to the audiences seated in their places. Here he was, for some reason, known as 'Harry'. He evidently became popular—he was a very pleasant man—and he even got his name on the 'bills' as an attraction, though there is no record that he actually performed. And the elders of the family, still children as they were, started to do jobs after school hours to help swell the exchequer. The Woods were doing pretty well by combining their efforts. Johnnie, the eldest son, got a job as an errand-boy, and he got such praise for this that it stung his sister, the mother-understudy, into action. She, Tilly, was not going to allow this sort of thing. She was not going to allow her juniors to get ahead of her. She announced that she too would earn some extra money. She was going on the stage. Her mother and father gazed at her. She announced that she had a chance of singing at the famous City Temple, for the no less famous Dr. Parker, its resident divine. She would not get any money then, she knew, but it would lead to other things. Young as she was, she realized that experience was necessary. She asked her mother to 'hear her piece' and to correct her faults; and her mother did so. And Tilly Wood started rehearsing the 'piece' which was to be her first success—she who in after-years was to be regarded as the last word in sauciness, spiciness, and naughtiness—broke into the entertainment world by means of a concert in a most famous nonconformist church, with a thing called 'Throw down the bottle and never drink again'.

She made an 'act' of this; she enlisted her sister Alice, who became a famous star, too; and these two children, who worked hard to get everything about their act perfectly right, did indeed score a big success. She formed her sister and a couple or so other children, who have left no mark on history, into the Fairy Bell Minstrels. The minstrel craze was at its height, and they were in great request. They had quite a repertory, but the final sketch, in the cause of temperance, was the high spot, with Alice as the wife of a drunkard and Marie, or Tilly, as the drunken husband. The high spot of that was Tilly's rendering of the dramatic renunciation, 'Throw down the bottle and never drink again'. Having tasted success, pretty little Tilly put on airs; she got a little wild and probably she got more than a little obnoxious at home. Success, even of the amateur kind, is a very heady vintage. She was getting near the time for leaving school; there was no legal school-leaving age then and no school certificate examinations. School was doing her no good; she was learning nothing, and she had no ideas about her own future at all. All she knew was that she wanted to go on the stage. And, even then, when there was so much more work than today and so many more places of amusement where stage work could be obtained, going on the stage was not so easy as all that. But her wise mother watched her. She saw the daughter was often roaming wild about the streets, making friends with all and sundry, seeing life as it could be seen in the very restricted circle of Hoxton and, incidentally, gathering experience of character and types which were to stand her in good stead later on. Mrs. Wood did not think her daughter in great danger, but she decided that some regular work would be good for her, so she applied on her daughter's behalf for a job for the girl in a factory where they made babies' boots. The manager, or proprietor, who knew her, agreed to give the girl an opening, and so Tilly was told that she now had a job. And Tilly did not like the sound of it at all. She could probably see her future shining before her, even though she had not yet found the gate whereby to enter. But they were a very happy family, the Woods, and at least she would be bringing home money to help them all. So she agreed. She started on Monday and she finished on Saturday. Making babies' boots was no good to her. She was a fish out of water, but her mother was determined. Work was the watchword of the family, as it was of all families in their position in those days. So again Mrs. Wood found her daughter a job; this time she was put to curling feathers. The only thing which she curled was her nose, and she left the job at the end of the week. But Mrs. Wood was not defeated, although the possibilities lessened. She went to the factory from which she drew the work which she herself did at home—trimming things with beads, not easy work, but demanding concentration and care, also creative ability. She got her daughter another chance. She made her an apron and bought her a pair of scissors and she sent her out again.

Now the worst thing which could happen, happened almost at once. The forewoman was a bit of a tyrant and she immediately disliked this golden-haired girl with her air of independence. She showed it, too, and that was a challenge to Tilly. She knew a lot of the girls who worked there and they knew all about her. They went the right way to work to make trouble. They knew she wanted to go on the stage.

They dared her to do a step-dance on the work-table. Tilly Wood was the last person to refuse a challenge. She obliged, to the delight and admiration of the girls. The forewoman returned, there was a short, sharp clash, and Tilly left the factory, then and there. She did not even bring away her apron and scissors. She had finished with that place. She was home in time for dinner at midday. She told her mother all about it, and her mother, for the first time, was despondent. 'Tilly, what are we going to do with you?' she sighed. 'Don't you worry, Mum,' replied Tilly, 'you don't have to do a thing. I'll do it all myself. I've been thinking. I've got it all worked out. I'm going to do what I want to do. I'm going on the stage—and I am going to call myself—Bella Delmore. . . .'

By the stage, Tilly, or Miss Bella Delmore, meant the Music Halls. They were in full flood. They were not confined to the West End, they were everywhere, and they were in Hoxton, too. Every district had its music hall, and supported it loyally. In many cases the Halls had not yet become entirely divorced from the public houses of their origin, and there was, very near where Tilly lived, a famous hall, whose memory lingers on in a famous jingle, 'Up and down the City Road, In and out the Eagle. . . .' The Eagle, a public house which had given birth to a most celebrated theatre, the Grecian, where many of the great ones had made their debut. It was an old-time place, even then. It was run on free-and-easy lines, and it had a chairman as master of ceremonies, but a very different person from the compère of today.

The compère is considered a modern idea imported from France by means of revue. Music Hall had him at its outset, only he was called The Chairman. He was a person of imposing appearance, who wore evening dress in a desert of ordinary clothes, had diamond studs in his shirt and diamond rings on his fingers—or at any rate they looked like diamonds. He had an unlimited capacity for the consumption of liquor which never upset his diction or his dignity or, indeed, his mastery of the situation. He sat at his table and ruled the proceedings. It was an honour to be allowed to sit with him and to buy him drinks and cigars. He could also sing a good song when occasion arose. He stood no nonsense, and when an audience got restive—as they did from time to time—he was always their master. The Music Halls of those days, and for years afterwards, did not worry themselves about taste in the matter of décor, what they wanted was warmth and what passed for splendour. So there was plenty of red plush and gold paint, plenty of light and plenty of glitter. That suited the audiences, who would have been at once repelled and subdued by pastel shades and delicacy of treatment. They wanted colour. and they got it; they wanted warmth, and they got it; their idea of splendour was just red plush and gilt.

Tilly Wood, alias Bella Delmore, got her first job at the Grecian, by the Eagle, in the City Road. How she got it is not on record, but her salary was fifteen shillings a week. Her mother made her stage costumes, and continued to do so for years.

She was fifteen years old. She had had no actual

experience, except as a child with her Fairy Bell
Minstrels. And she entered upon a form of entertainment which was 'sudden death'. For on the
Halls you had to capture an audience right away
or your number, which had just gone up, was
down again. One does not know if she had ever
been back-stage at a music hall of those days
before. If not, the moment that she did so, she
must have suffered the disillusionment which comes
to every beginner when they enter the stage door
for the first time. For the stage door is not the
gateway to romance which so many people imagine
it to be. It is the workman's entrance—the trades-
man's entrance, up a back alley, dark, dismal, and in
the 1880's invariably dirty, too. Back-stage conditions then would appal the pampered 'pros' of today,
when theatres have such things as lifts, hot and cold
running water, comfortable, well-furnished dressing-
rooms and even baths. There were no such things
then. Dressing-rooms had bare, damp walls, and if
you wanted to wash—well, there was the bucket. You
had to be strong, you had to have the madness of
the theatre (which includes the Music Hall), you
had to have supreme confidence in your own powers
and you had to have attack, to fight that enemy
which faced you every night; for every audience is a
performer's enemy, Theatre or Music Hall. One or
other has to win. Bella Delmore knew that instinctively. But she knew little else. She did not know that
you had to have songs which were your own
property, that you could not sing songs belonging to
other people. So she sang what she liked. Nobody

knows exactly how her first turn at the Grecian went. But she could not have been a 'flop'. That was not in her, nor in her stars. She got jobs, though she probably got no more money than that first salary of fifteen shillings. The days of big salaries were yet to come. But she took another step along the road which was to bring her to fame and fortune and immortality. She had not yet found her true line. She was a 'song and dance' act like so many others. She had no song of her own, to suit her own talent and personality, and probably she did not know, as yet, in what direction that lay. But still, this pretty, very attractive girl, with the bright, shining blue eyes, the golden hair and the twinkle, got by all right, although she did not knock them out of their seats and get an increase in salary. There was even then something about her which pleased. She was so bright and gay. She was already shedding that radiance about her, subdued as yet, for she did not know the mechanics, but it was there. She had made the mistake which many people have made, before and since, in the choice of her stage name. She had gone all out for something which she thought grand and romantic. She did not know that a simple name, one easy to remember, was the best. In the rank and file of music hall at all times and in the same humble positions in the minor posts of the theatre, one found the grand names, smacking of heroes and heroines of the novelettes, aiming at the flavour of France and missing it by miles. Bella Delmore did not mean a thing, there were hundreds with similar names. An astute manager told her. She had got an interview with him and he was discussing the possibility of work with her. His seeing eye had spotted, what the public had already spotted, a star in the making. Here was charm and personality. Here was talent and attack which was instinctive. Here was all the parts of the engine which needed only proper assembling to make the steepest grade which now led to the summit, the top of the bill. And very wisely, he thought little of her stage name, that rather pompous and utterly unlikely Bella Delmore.

He asked her what her real name was, and she told him 'Tilly Wood'. Well, he did not like that, even though he thought it better than Bella Delmore. Anyway, it was not his job to give her a stage christening. But he could and did give her good advice. 'Go away and do a bit of thinking,' he said. 'Get rid of Bella Delmore, she won't get you anywhere. Think of a short name—two short names—which go together easily so that people can remember them. Short names are better than long names, and real names which people know and frequently use are better than fantastic names which they can never remember. Choose for yourself, but keep it short and keep it familiar.' Tilly Wood—Bella Delmore—went away and considered. She had always liked the name Marie—pronounced Mahry—and it was almost a nickname of hers now. That would do for one. But what about the other—a short name, a common name which people knew and could remember. She found it difficult to decide on that. Probably she regretted the death of Bella Delmore, which stood in her mind as romantic, but she had already learnt that

romance had no place in Music Hall. What was
wanted was something homely and down-to-earth,
something which was really of the people, something
which had nothing 'lah-di-dah' about it. Not only
then was this so, but also much later, for one
remembers a young man of refined appearance and
manners, clad in a very well-cut dinner-jacket being
told at the respectable Crouch End Hippodrome to
'Get orf—we don't want toffs here.' It must be
homely, she thought. She worried about it, maybe
she asked for advice, but that was unlikely, as she
mostly made her own decisions. And then, quite
suddenly and in the street, inspiration came.

It came in the form of a big poster on the walls,
what is known to advertising people as a *forty-eight
sheet pictorial*. That poster bore a picture of an old
gentleman in his shirt-sleeves, with a circular
smoking-cap on his grey hair and a kindly, if rather
superior, expression on his face. His right hand was
raised in admonition, the index-finger extended; he
was evidently laying down the law and giving people
the benefit of his wisdom, whether they wanted it or
not. The caption was 'The Family Oracle', and in his
left hand he held the source of the information he
could impart. It was the fountain of all the wisdom
which he was prepared to disclose; in his opinion it
was quite infallible. That encyclopædia of knowledge
was a newspaper and its name was *Lloyds Weekly
News*. The name screamed at you in enormous type.
Tilly-Bella saw it and was riveted to the spot. She
gasped. There it was. And it fitted so well with
Marie. Marie Lloyd—that was the name; and from

that moment onwards Marie Lloyd she was. So great things happen, so does inspiration come. That family oracle had, for once, been dead right. He had given the world a name which was to lighten it for years. A name to be remembered. He had named an immortal. He had given Marie Lloyd the name which was to take her to the very top of the bill.

III

THE UPWARD JOURNEY

THE journey by Marie Lloyd to the coveted position at the top of the bill was rapid. There was no influence behind her, no friend at court. She had only that vivid personality, that tremendous talent, that ability to control an audience and to make them like her. There was that thing which was, perhaps, her chief asset—her radiance. For this girl seemed to shine. Her eyes shone, her hair shone, her teeth shone. It was in her smile, her face, her hands, her feet, everywhere. She shone brighter than any lamps which exhibited her name. She was like the sunshine on a fine spring morning. She did not, of course, get into the big money right away. There was not much big money in the Music Halls in the eighties. That Grand Old Man of Music Hall, Bill Boardman, has verified that Marie Lloyd was paid fifteen shillings a week at the Star, Bermondsey, in March 1885.

Marie had not yet got her own songs. Quite unconsciously she 'pinched' the songs of others. She meant no harm, she knew nothing of business, of 'sole performing rights'; to her, a song was a song, something to sing and, if she liked it, well, she sang it. She was, of course, still only fifteen, and she had not got near the West End, so little attention was paid to this unconscious piracy. But suddenly the blow fell. Somebody got to hear, and she was threatened with an injunction. She did not know what it meant, but it sounded awful, and she was scared stiff. The crime was explained, and she humbly apologized. She promised never to do it again; she swore that next week she would have her own songs. And somehow she got them. Where they came from one does not know, but there were hundreds of song-writers then who lived most precarious lives, writing to order, or by inspiration. They sold their songs literally for 'a song'. Five pounds was big money for them, many of them, and there was no question of a royalty. They sold outright. They watched artistes and wrote songs in their manner. They wrote them in pubs, on the backs of envelopes or on bits of paper, and somehow they made a living. A few, of course, who were wiser and perhaps more provident than the others, made a good deal of money, but not the rank and file. These makers of songs, who contributed so much to the gaiety of the nation and the fortunes of the singers who sang their ballads, lived from hand to mouth. Some would advertise in the *Stage, Era, The Encore,* and other papers read by the profession. They were extraordinary advertisements, offering 'part rights' of 'side-splitters and screamers' for five shillings; £1 bought the sole rights. So Marie Lloyd would not have had much difficulty in getting songs. But there was one which she sang very early on, which Nellie Power, another great performer, also sang, and it was called *The Boy I Love Sits up in the Gallery.* It was a big success with Marie Lloyd, for not only the boys in the gallery, but the boys all over the hall were in love with her; and, strange as it

may seem, the women loved her too. Even at that
early age, they recognized her as a brilliant representative of their sex, a sort of champion, doing all
the things they would like to do, wearing the clothes
they would like to wear. There was never any
jealousy in their hearts, for she was no stuck-up
madam, this girl. They knew that she was one of
themselves.

She was not to remain in the semi-obscurity of
the East End Halls for any time at all. She was
getting talked about. She was always a success, and
already a reputation for naughtiness was growing
up round her, and that, in her line, was a very
useful asset. Yet, despite that reputation which
still persists, she never in all her career sang what
was known as a 'dirty' song, or a line which was
really 'blue'. Proof of it is extant—her songs can be
examined—and there is no trace of this suggested
salacity. Vulgarity, yes, but that honest vulgarity of
the Music Halls, of the public houses, of the ordinary
people themselves. It must be recorded that she had
most expressive hands, a most expressive face and
eyes, and a perfect mastery of nods, becks, wreathed
smiles and winks, and her winks were jet-propelled
and armour-piercing! But she left it entirely to you.
To what you chose to think: she never said it at all.
Smutty stories were foisted on her, most of which
originated in that incubator of such things, the Stock
Exchange. 'Heard Marie Lloyd's latest,' men would
say. And then they would recount what was in those
days referred to as a smoking-concert story. But
Marie had never told that tale, and more than

probably she had never heard it. A woman who was of such bodily cleanliness did not have a mind which created filth. Sauciness, yes—a suggestion or two—yes; but it was her audience who supplied what they wanted to believe. One or two of the stories about her die hard. She is credited with a remark about a traffic hold-up in the Strand. She never said it. She is reputed to have sung a song concerning a market garden and its contents—nobody has yet been found who ever heard her do so—nor is the song on record. But she acquired that reputation even in her earliest days and, professionally, it did her little harm, save on one important occasion, which will be dealt with in its place. There was another occasion, too, when it won her a great victory . . . but that is another story yet awhile. But there she was, in 1885, at the age of fifteen—a success and going up the ladder fast. She got to the old Oxford Music Hall in the West End the same year in which she started her career.

At the Oxford, she sang a sentimental song, and she followed it with a dance that was known as a skirt dance. It was danced with long, accordion-pleated skirts. And that girl could dance with lightness and grace, they said. The Oxford was a famous Music Hall. It has gone now, like so many places of happy memories. A date at the Oxford ensured that you were seen by everybody, agents and managers as well as the general Music Hall public. It stood on part of the site now covered by Messrs. Lyons Corner House at the Tottenham Court Road end of Oxford Street, and it had been founded by the Father of Music Hall, Charles Morton himself. It was, indeed, the first real

Music Hall to be built within the charmed circle of the West End of London. Only just within it, true, but it was really West End. Morton had come to it from the Canterbury, and had made it immensely popular. He filled it with stars, and he had a restaurant attached, at which you could have, in addition to seeing the show, a table d'hôte consisting of soup, fish, entrée, vegetables, salad, sweet, and bread and cheese, the whole thing for half a crown. And both food and entertainment were of the best. The drinks were of fine quality, and cheap as well.

The Oxford was all of Music Hall in its four walls, and Marie had reached it within a few months of her start. Fame she acquired, fortune of a sort she acquired, and some bursts of happiness. But on the whole, despite her tremendous popularity and world-wide appeal, she did not really know much genuine, lasting happiness. In that first twelve months, follow-ing the Oxford, she got a date in Ireland. She got £10 a week, and that first fifteen shillings had grown and multiplied. She could afford to buy songs now. She could afford a brougham in which to drive from hall to hall, when she played more than one a night. And £10 a week was quite a lot of money in those spacious days. The brougham would cost her £2 a week—inclusive of the driver, who would be one of those men who drove the pros from one hall to another and were a race apart. They knew their job, and they knew their customers. They knew the best way between each hall and they knew the times at which their fares had to appear at each. They knew everything, even just how long they could afford to wait at a tavern about half-way for the harmless, necessary drink. And like everything else connected with the Music Halls, they were efficient. They never let you down. And Marie could afford that now, and she could also afford her own house, which she had rented in the suburbs and into which she moved her family. It is to be feared that the quick, sudden success and the money, in sums previously beyond the dreams of her family, had turned her head. But perhaps that is not the right word. She had no conceit, she was never given to what is called swank. The money she earned enabled her to have pretty clothes, which she loved, good food, which she loved, and, better still, to give her family a good time. Those of her sisters who wanted to follow in her footsteps—and several of them did—Alice, Gracie, Rosie, and Daisy—could now have tuition which she herself had never received. Also, it enabled her to give generously—far too generously—to almost everyone who came to ask her help. Ask they did, but she never turned them away. But when a girl has seen her salary rise from six half-crowns a week to £10 and then to £100 a week in a remarkably short space of time, the prospects seem limitless.

She had got her own songs now and she no longer sang those written for others. She had, of course, kept her word about that, and keeping her promise was one of her strong points. Those songs were giving delight, but what gave much more delight was the way she sang them. Here was a girl who was very pretty indeed in her own way, who sparkled with life and vitality, who had an aura of mischief and who

was the very spirit of London. Here was a smile
which dazzled and a personality which just compelled attention and gave off brightness and excitement. Always she was exciting. It was one of her
chief assets.

It is not possible, nor is it desirable to write a
book about her which is just a list of facts: of 'dates'
she played, of towns she visited, of what happened to
her and of all those details which go to make the
sum of the ordinary book about a theatrical star.
That is all right in the case of an actress or actor, but
it cannot be done in the case of a Music Hall performer. They had no background of plays, no yardstick of gradual perfection in their art. It is not
possible to say that here, at such a date definite steps
forward were made—there, at another time in that
part, greatness was first shown. In this play, failure.
In that play, success. For the Music Hall performer
was an individualist—relying entirely upon himself
or herself. It did not matter much where they played,
they were the central figures in their own story. There
did not come a day when they were engaged by
Irving, Tree, or Alexander. There was no gradual
progress from the chorus of the touring musical
comedy to a leading part at the Gaiety Theatre in
town. Nothing of that kind. Their story was their
own. They were always on the move, so they
collected little stability or background in any town.
Nor did they get publicity, for they 'opened' on
Monday and were gone on Saturday. Their 'graph',
as it were, was their position on the bill. And their
position in the programme, which mattered a good

deal. They would begin in small type. Their billing would get larger and, in due course, become 'middle of the bill', and that was the third most important position. There many of them became stuck. The better could then graduate to 'bottom of the bill', which was second stardom, and there a great many more stuck. Or they could rocket to 'top of the bill', and that the elect did, the chosen few out of the hundreds, nay, thousands of performers.

And as a rule, those who became 'tops' did not take long to get there, because it was really public acclaim which put them there. As individualists they made their appeal, and the public either acclaimed them or not. If the verdict was in the affirmative, up they went. They stayed there by their own efforts, just so long as the public came to see them. Any stage performer may—usually does—rise by degrees, but in the case of the star Music Hall performer it was usually a pretty swift affair because of the almost instant impact on the public, who were, and who always are, the arbiters of success. And although there are cases where performers have changed their lines and found success at the second venture, they were few. Harry Tate was one. He was a mimic and a good one. He was middle of the bill before he started his amazing sketches with 'Motoring'. He was perhaps the best character comedian of all time, and he went to the top with a bang. He had been a star as a mimic and a good pantomime performer. He was one of the best 'Abanazars' ever seen, but it was 'Motoring'—and the moustache—which put him top of the bill. Bransby Williams was a mimic, too, but his Dickens characters really made him. With others, it was a song which swept them to that coveted top position.

But with Marie Lloyd it was entirely herself, the whole of her and her essential, inherent talent and utter femininity. Don't mistake that word for meaning refinement, or for being what was then called 'genteel' or ladylike behaviour. It had nothing to do with that. Nor had it anything to do with what is now referred to as 'sex'. She had sex appeal, of course, but it was a different appeal from the sort which is trailed so openly today. Here was no slinky charmer, here was no girl exploiting physical measurements and feminine appendages; here was no suggestion of scented, perfumed nights of sensuous licence. Her appeal was as a woman, a straightforward, jolly woman, who was above all else a pal. A woman of the world, with worldly knowledge, who patently enjoyed life without the necessary intrusion of lust or sex at all. Here was a woman who would be the life and soul of the party and yet hold the men enthralled without upsetting the women. Here was the very embodiment of that woman who was the veneration of the males and the respected, if envied, ideal of the females. She was of that class which was the backbone of Music Hall, the lower middle and the working classes. Marie Lloyd was the woman who would be the ideal wife for the *fully licensed man*—the landlord of the pub, which was every man and every woman's club of that stratum of society. She was the hearty, fresh, handsome woman of great understanding, hail-fellow-well-met, to whom hats would be raised and hands waved as she and her 'old man', or as they would have said 'her old pot and pan', flashed by on a fine Sunday morning in the smart dog-cart with the well-moving pony en route for Chingford and Epping Forest, Burnham Beeches, or Hampton Court. Always she was one of them-selves—never aloof. That she could and did make her audience of men chuckle and wink—as she winked at them—and the ladies giggle and pretend to be shocked, was most true. But it was always the idea which she suggested, but never mentioned, which made them do so rather than any illicit desire for her themselves. That was why she was 'Our Marie'—one of themselves, belonging to them, not something from what they felt was a higher class. She could illustrate their lives because that was just the life she knew, and she saw other characters, put in to add variety to her extensive repertoire. The chic Frenchwoman, the lady in the Directoire skirt, and lots of others, just as they saw them. That was true of so many idols of the Halls, but never more true than of Marie Lloyd.

And above all her radiance pierced their gloom and wiped away their troubles. However downcast they had been when they went to see her, she put them on the upgrade and was a tonic. No wonder they shouted 'Good old Marie'—even when she was a young girl. That 'old' was the English word of endearment. She never portrayed romance, she never went in for passion. It is doubtful if she created much desire. It was typical of the girl who had bathed the babies and done the housework, yet found

time to sing at church bazaars with her eyes on her
ultimate goal. She was a person of gaiety, of light. She
was to have her dark passages and many of them.
But she never expected anyone else to share in those.

The dark women of the world, the *femmes fatales,*
the type which came to be called 'vamps' when
exploited on the screen, were as nothing to her in
their own genius. They had to rely upon artificial
aids. They needed a special background to their
sinister sinuosity. Dim lights, flowing draperies of a
diaphanous type, heady perfumes, and silken couches,
maybe leopard- or tiger-skins. Marie needed none of
that. Give her a front cloth in 'one'—that is, right
down stage, just a narrow strip of stage on which to
work, give her the band and an audience, and she
was the best beloved. She did it herself. And she did
good by bringing joy into the world.

Whenever an old Music Hall dies, and is given over
to the house-breakers, it becomes news for a day or
two, and always in the stories printed you will find it
stated that Marie Lloyd played there. Of course she
did. She played everywhere, or almost everywhere, all
over the country. The only Music Hall of any note
at which there is no record of her appearing was the
London Coliseum. That may seem odd, but there is
probably a reason for it. When Sir Oswald Stoll
(plain Mr. Stoll then) took it over, he began a new
system. He went all out for 'refinement'. He wanted
a place where the 'young person' would not have a
blush brought to those damask and easily flushed
cheeks, he wanted an essentially family house where
maiden aunts could be taken, where the whole family

could meet the vicar and not be nonplussed. He achieved that, too. And although he had plenty of Music Hall acts in his astounding programmes—the Coliseum started with four shows a day—Marie Lloyd was never one, not then nor at any future time. She was probably considered 'not the thing' for such audiences. The discipline which was brought to bear on 'keeping the party clean' was quite amazing. A list of rules hung in every dressing-room and heavy penalties were exacted for a slip. Artistes had to 'clean up' their acts for the Coliseum, and not even a mild 'damn' was allowed. It is much to be feared that Marie would not have taken it seriously. The rebel in her would have been aroused. She would have regarded this as 'blank' nonsense, and the blank would have been trenchant and expressive. So she did not play there. Later she was well on the other side in the Music Hall strike, in direct opposition to Sir Oswald Stoll. So perhaps the omission from then on was understandable. Yet, properly handled, she would have shed a much-needed radiance on those Coliseum bills, which were, it must be admitted, a trifle stodgy at times, although always excellent in quality. When the great theatre, as it now is, celebrated its jubilee recently, none of those who paid it a tribute mentioned the fact that Marie Lloyd had *not* played there. The point is well worthy of notice; it is on a par with the number of places at which Queen Elizabeth is said to have slept, and, in America, where George Washington passed the night. There is an establishment in Broadstairs, the Kent seaside resort, which boldly announces on its front

that Charles Dickens never wrote a word there or
stayed there. Surely a plaque should be affixed to the
Coliseum saying that Marie Lloyd never played
there. It is fame in the oblique.

Marie in her teens was a star, ranking with the
great ones. She had still some way to go before she
was 'Our Marie'. She was not yet the idol. She had
not reached maturity in years or in art. But that
Music Hall public, which had such a discerning eye,
had spotted her. She had not yet got the songs which
have lived, and that is part of the heritage of greatness for a Music Hall performer. It was the chorus
songs which made them stars, which were the un-
breakable links which held them grappled to the
public. Marie's early songs are not too well remembered. She had sung that song of Nellie Power's—*The
Boy I Love Sits up in the Gallery,* and they had liked
that because there again was the democratic link—
she did not love a 'swell', a 'masher', a 'toff'—which
were the words used then for what afterwards became
the 'k'nuts' and 'socialites'. She was, you see, true to
her class. She had made a big impression with that
'Boy in the Gallery' song at the Middlesex Music Hall
in Drury Lane—the old 'Mo' (a shortened form of
'Mogul') which had, of course, been the public house
from which the Hall sprang. At that same Hall Dan
Leno had discovered that he was an even better
comedian than he was a clog-dancer, and he was
champion of England at clog-dancing. The old Mo
is no more, nor is the Middlesex, but the Winter
Garden Theatre stands on its site. Well, Marie Lloyd
did play there, and with great success.

The songs were beginning. The ones which could be quickly learned and remembered and whistled. For that was the great test. The whistling of the errand-boy and the music of the piano-organ—that was the yardstick of popularity whilst Marie Lloyd was in her teens. It was a time when songs lasted, instead of the few weeks they last now before radio tears them to tatters by over-use and saturation.

IV

MARIE—WIFE, MOTHER, AND STAR

ONE of the great drawbacks from which Marie Lloyd suffered was that quality which also made her a star. She seldom, if ever, stopped to think. That cheery, go-ahead, take-what-comes-and-make-the-best-of-it attitude was part of the radiance which she disseminated to such a degree. Everything she did on the stage seemed to be impromptu, the inspiration of the minute and not a studied act. She acted on the inspiration of the minute too often in her own life, and nearly always to her detriment. If she had had a strong manager who could have controlled her in some way, have handled her affairs and taken care of that vast stream of money which flowed in so fast and so steadily; which flowed out again just as fast and just as steadily, much of the grief she knew could have been spared her. But then, she would not have been Marie Lloyd. Naturally, she was what the world called a Bohemian. And the citizens or lieges of the land of Bohemia make their own laws. That is what makes them Bohemians. Today the picture of a Bohemian is often that of an unkempt person of either sex, with ill-kept hair, dirty finger-nails, ridiculous clothes, and drunken habits. Real Bohemians are not like that at all. They are usually people who are very clean and dress well, who live well, and don't get drunk, at least habitually. They do not obey conventions, but they have conventions of their own. They are decent, law-abiding people and a credit to the community, for the Bohemianism is within them and needs no outward show. They have what is called 'the artistic temperament', and they really do have it, not like the people who are boorish and rude and get excused their churlishness because they have 'temperament'. The artistic temperament of a Bohemian disregards what is the usual daily round of business and commercial routine, believes that its own form of art is the only one that matters, and also believes in having a good time and giving others a good time. Nor does Bohemianism include immorality, and many of the best Bohemians lead and led perfectly impeccable private lives, as ideal husbands, wives, mothers and fathers. It simply means one part of the world of illusion of which Bohemia is a province.

Marie Lloyd was a native of that delectable land which has become so circumscribed during recent years. A girl of seventeen, a popular favourite, tasting nightly the heady wine of applause, flattery and adulation, handling sums of money which a couple of years before would have seemed to her only possible in the case of the Rothschilds. Of course Marie lost her head. She did nothing fatally foolish. Maybe she had her flirtations, her little affaires, yet in the main she was a moral woman, with her own code of morality, but not a bad one at that. To her, money was nothing, except that it could be spent, and except that it could give pleasure. That was what she always wanted to do, and what she did. Her family benefited and, as has been stated, she encouraged them to take the path she had chosen. Well, why not, she thought. I'm all right, they are my brothers and sisters, so why not they? They are Lloyds, too. They were not—they were Woods. But nearly all had a try, and some of them succeeded. Alice Lloyd was a delightful woman, a very pretty one and an excellent artiste. She was overshadowed by her remarkable sister, but at least she avoided many of that sister's mistakes. And there was Daisy, who was also a fine artiste. But she did not take her sister's name. She was Daisy Wood. Marie even got them into a musical sketch called 'The Bond Street Tea Walk'. Some of them became double turns, some stuck to single acts, but all those who continued to remain in 'the profession' did well on their own merits. They did not copy their great sister, except in the name. There is much of interest in the careers of Alice, Gracie, Rosie, Daisy, Annie, Sid, and Maudie, but there is no space here for it to be chronicled. Here the limelight must rest on one of them alone, Marie.

Marie as a child had never recked the cost, and as a young successful girl she did not do so either. She was headstrong and impulsive. She took people and things at their face value. If she liked them, they were all right; she made no inquiries about them. They were all right with her, unless and until she found them out. That worked out in many ways. She never looked for ulterior motives, she did not know what they meant. She was too quick in her own feelings and far too generous-hearted to look for calculation in others. But she made mistakes. She had a benefit when she had been on the stage almost no time at all. It was suggested to her by a gentleman in her profession, who knew about such things. She was delighted, and he arranged it for her on terms which he explained, but which she never troubled to examine. She was not swindled, but the arranger did as well, if not better than she did herself. That, of course, had been the reason for his suggestion. She threw herself into the affair with that enormous gusto which was part of her and it was a great success. Benefits were usual in those days, everybody had them, they were indeed still part of an artiste's income, although they were gradually dying out as salaries increased.

The benefit, held at the Oxford Music Hall, was a big success. And most of what she got out of it she spent in the most characteristic fashion. She bought eighty pairs of boots and shoes, half for boys and half for girls, for the children at the school in Hoxton where she had been a scholar—and not the brightest or the best-behaved. It was typical of her. She might have invested the money, she might have bought jewels or furs or new clothes, she might have given some to charity or have thrown a grand party. She did none of those things—she gave boots to children who needed them, and she knew the need. She could always see the need in others, but never the need in herself. She was, from the very outset of her career, the gift from God to the mumper, the beggar, the 'screever' or begging-letter writer. She just could not say 'No'. They would besiege her and pour out their tale of woe. She would listen for a few moments; she never had time to listen to the whole tale, there was always so much to do, and if she liked their looks, they would get largesse full measure and brimming over. It was the same with those who wrote asking for help. If something about the opening of the letter rang true to her, they got what they asked. To the more needy of her own profession, she was a Lady Bountiful, and she was one of those blessed people, too, who gave before being asked, if she thought the need was real. If one of them was in trouble, she would move heaven and earth. There was a minor artiste who often was on the same bill with her whom she once found in tears. She took her to her dressing-room and wanted to know all about it. The girl told Marie that she was going to have a baby. Whether she was married or not does not matter here and did not matter to Marie. The girl had been told that, as her 'condition' was becoming apparent, there would be no more 'dates' until the 'happy event' was over and done with. The girl saw disaster ahead. Marie went into action at once. To her, this seemed like tyranny, a thing she could not endure. She saw to it that the girl got some clothes made at once, and at Marie's expense, which would disguise that 'condition' as long as possible, and she got into touch with the managements who had contracts with the girl, begging them to let her work on as long as possible, as the money would be wanted for the baby. She got her way and she saw to it that the girl was looked after when the time came. She would say nothing about this to anyone, and to her it was just the

natural thing. Somebody wanted help—you had the
means—so, of course, you gave the help. She must
have given away a fortune in her time to some who
were deserving, but to many more who were not.
Nobody could have stopped her, although a firm
hand might have curbed and could have kept the
wolves away from their all too willing victim.

She acted on impulses. She liked adoration and
flattery. She liked people to like her, and she was
too easily swayed. So, like many other girls of
seventeen, she fell in love, or believed she did, with
a man considerably her senior. She had met him
the year before. He was a handsome man with
excellent manners, a courtly form of address; a bright,
cheerful fellow to the outside world. He impressed
her very much. He was different: not like the familiar,
down-to-earth men of her own calling, or those whom
she met in the course of her social life. She never
went into 'society' because that was unheard of in
her day. She met the people of her own type and
class. Good chaps, hail-fellow-well-met, laughing,
joking, bonhomous men with hearty laughs and
rowdy ideas. Men who liked their drink and their
steaks and chops, men who were publicans, tradesmen, sporting and racing types. Some were
journalists, and, of course, some the Music Hall
fraternity, managerial and artistic. Mr. Courtney was
not like that. He seemed to be that oddity which
nobody ever likes to name 'a gentleman'. He had an
air and a way with him. He was a little superior to
all the others. He might even have been 'a bit above'
her in class, yet she knew he was not. But he courted

her with swiftness and ardour and he swept her off
her feet. She fell in love with all the warmth of a
young girl, pleased and proud that somebody who
was evidently a man of the world with considerable
experience should want her for his wife. For it came
to that when he proposed to her. She did not stop to
think. She accepted him. If she had thought, she
would have remembered that she had met him in
entirely her own surroundings, at the old Forester's
Music Hall—never a resort of the aristocracy or even
the gentlefolk. Not that there is anything to prove
that Percy Courtney ever suggested he was any better
than she, but he seemed so. If she had stopped to
think, she might have wondered what he did for a
living. He seemed to be always at the Music Halls,
wherever she was, anyway. Yet he was not a performer. He always seemed to have money and he
never seemed to mind spending it. She never stopped
to consider what was his profession, how he lived, or
how his calling would fit in with hers, or whether he
had any means of livelihood at all. Why should she?
It did not matter to her. At a time when women had
no 'rights' such as they enjoy now, when ladies of
the middle and upper classes had not the independence of action which they have today, she *had* those
things because she was a Bohemian and a Music
Hall star. Independent because she was famous, but
chiefly because she earned a splendid income, the
idea of his being 'able to support her', which was
regarded as essential in the Victorian years, did
not arise. She was young, she was rich, she was in
love. It was enough. Marie Lloyd married Percy

Courtney when she had reached the mature age of seventeen.

Mr. Courtney was a man of leisure. There was no real harm in him. He did no work, he followed no trade and profession, but such money as he made, he got by backing horses. That was his idea of life. It had excitement, it had thrill, and although it was not a reliable means of income, he got along. Soon he was the husband of a girl who was already well known and who was obviously going to be very famous indeed. He was the husband of a girl who enjoyed a very big income and who was the favourite of vast sections of the public. He could, of course, be her business manager—a very desirable, if slightly onerous, occupation. Not hard work, for he would be selling something in great demand, but onerous because he would himself, he, the male and the one who should be the predominate partner, always be definitely No. 2. He would have little or no identity. He would be Mr. Marie Lloyd. To his lot would fall attendance in the dressing-room, the arguments with agents and managers, the hanging about the bars in the Halls whilst his wife played. He would, as 'the profession' calls it, 'carry the band-parts'. He would have to attend the inevitable 10 a.m. call at the Hall every Monday morning, with those band-parts. He would have to lay them along the footlights and wait for the musical director, the 'Mus. Dir.' of Halls, to call out the name, and then explain what was wanted. If a new number, he would have it run through and he would be there, too, when his wife sang it over and rehearsed with the band. He would have to look after the household accounts and do most of the things wives generally did. He would always, always be a very second fiddle. Against that, there was the reflected glory from his wife's fame and a pretty good living from the income. It would be untrue to say that Mr. Courtney was actuated by sordid means, that he married Marie Lloyd because he wanted to live upon her earnings. There is absolutely nothing to prove that or suggest it. And there is every reason in the world to believe that he was in love with her, a victim of that radiance and charm and sparkle. She was in love with him, there is no doubt about that. The wedding was celebrated in sumptuous fashion— with a joyous wedding breakfast, lots of champagne and jokes and fun, and heartfelt good wishes from everyone. They took a house in Lewisham, a very nice house in a good road at a good rental. And if Mr. Courtney had expected that the onus of looking after that house would fall on him, he was soon to have his eyes opened. His wife's pride in personal cleanliness did not stop there. It extended to everything round her. She had been brought up to work. She had helped her mother, who took pride in her house, and she had a pride in the house she now possessed. She looked into every detail. She supervised the servants. Woe betide the girl who swept dust under the mats or under the beds. She was discovered and fired. Marie Lloyd looked into things herself. Woe betide the housemaid who only dusted what could be seen. Marie's bright blue eyes saw through everything. Woe betide her, too, if she did not keep the cupboards and corners as clean as everywhere else. Marie was always on the scout for dirt. And she had no mercy at all on bad workers or on sluts. She was accustomed to giving her best and she demanded it from others. And she got it, too. For most of the women who worked for her, if they were not wholly beyond hope, just adored her.

In due course, a baby arrived—a little daughter. And Marie was happy and proud, and there is no doubt that Mr. Courtney shared her feelings. Marie adored that child. She could not stay away from work for very long. One of the penalties of being a Music Hall star is that one must give personal service and not disappoint a public. A star performer must have no private life, for the public is as selfish in one way as it can be generous in another. It demands what it wants, and if that cannot be supplied, it sets up another idol. It wanted Marie Lloyd, and she had to be there. So the baby, which was christened Marie after her mother, was brought to her at the Hall in which she worked, or the nearest to her home if she was working at several. Sometimes the baby would even accompany her on her journey from one to another because Marie had determined to be a 'real mother' to the mite and to feed her herself. Many women in her profession would not have considered that for a moment, but here was motherliness and a maternal instinct very highly developed. That baby, in due course, grew up to be very like her wonderful mother, to become a performer, and in due course to sing the songs the mother sang, and, of course, to bear her name. If, perhaps, she never became so great a star as the original Marie Lloyd—well, there was only one Marie Lloyd and there could not be another who was as great—it is a natural law. But Marie was happy. She had all that she needed: a husband, a baby, a home, a carriage—and popularity. Maybe the last-named was her greatest joy.

She entertained lavishly, as did all the Music Hall stars. She gave parties on Sunday nights at her Lewisham home when she was performing in town and not prevented by long train journeys between one 'date' and another. And everyone who was any-one in the world of Music Hall, or any of the branches thereof, were always delighted to come to those parties. You would see them all at Marie's, and entertainments were given that no manager could have afforded to stage and no public could have paid for. But Marie's time was the very peak period of the Halls. She lived in a generation of giants, none of which surpassed her in stature, which it is as well to remember when picturing her in the mind. All those stars who were in town would be there and delighted to be with her. Nobody was jealous of Marie. You might meet Arthur Lennard, Marie Collins, Marie Kendal, Lottie Collins, Tom Bass, the brothers Griffith, Lily Burnand (Lovely Lively Lily Burnand was her 'bill matter'), Katie Lawrence, R. G. Knowles, Harry Randall, Herbert Campbell, and the great and one and only Dan Leno himself.

Those Sunday nights were a regular thing in Music Hall land, and their like does not exist today. They all kept open house, and sometimes guests would go from one to another. The Sunday night parties of dear old Kate Carney, when she lived at Brixton with her husband, George Barclay, were something to see and at which to wonder. Mr. Barclay, a man of great business talent, a star-maker indeed, a racehorse owner, a gambler of great discernment on the turf, quite fearless and with an independence all his own, was the host, and his methods were forceful rather than in the tradition of 'the best people'. What he thought, he said. If he did not like the way a thing was done, he took action. He would throw the food downstairs at the cook if it were not up to his high standard. But you were always welcome, and there was the hostess, large and smiling, in great finery and literally ablaze with jewels. With great gentility she wore gloves on these occasions, but there was no need for such good breeding to interfere with the proper enjoyment by herself and all beholders of the many and handsome rings which she possessed. So, with a simple and quite unselfconscious regality, she wore them over her gloves. Everybody was satisfied and a wonderful time was had by all.

It was not quite that at Marie's parties. To begin with, she had excellent taste. She knew about clothes, she knew what became her and how to wear it. And she had good taste in furniture. She knew a good 'piece' when she saw it. If she liked it a bit ornate, all right; why not? If the more colourful periods and styles appealed to her; again, why not? But there was no bad taste, no shocking clashes, no mixing of rubbish with quality. She had an instinct in these things.

At these parties, Mr. Courtney would be host. He had little to do: he saw that everyone got all they wanted and that the gentlemen had cigars and a glass.

He was not in great request. He was in it, but not
really of it. He made the best of it, but it was Marie
they came to see. He knew them all and they knew
him, but the freemasonry of the Halls is even
greater, or perhaps one should say, was even greater
than that of the theatre. If the 'legits' of those days
were in a world apart, they lay nearer the frontiers
of reality than did the Music Hall 'Ohmès'. For these
good folk were absolutely absorbed in their work
and in their individuality. They spoke what was
almost a language of their own amongst themselves.
They spoke rhyming slang and a curious mixture of
Romany and ordinary speech, quite unintelligible to
a stranger or layman, but perfectly clear to themselves. If one told another that he had 'no medals',
he was understood to be hard up. You did not run
away, you 'scarpered'. And a pro in low water might
be guilty, by force of circumstances, of 'scarpering
the letty', which meant that he had vacated his dig-
gings without paying the bill. They ate supper at
Marie's, for late dinner meant nothing to them. There
would be good and plain fare and lots of it. For
instance, there might be some 'stop thief on the Cain
and Abel', and many came to the party in a 'flounder
and dab' along the 'frog and toad', and maybe called
in at the 'rub-a-dub' for a half-pint of 'pigs' en route.
And they would say just that. They never went to
bed, it was 'Uncle Ned' who claimed the rest hours,
with their heads on the 'weeping willow' whilst they
took a little 'Bo-Peep'. And when they came to
Marie's 'Rory O'More' they were in for a good time
and knew it.

Everybody spoke at once, everybody talked at the tops of their voices—they had to be heard at all costs, and if the laughter was loud and boisterous, it was quite genuine. But there was real silence if one of them performed, and there was always a concert at the end, when sometimes new songs designed to make Music Hall history were tried out for the first time to the most critical audience. Always the applause was generous and full-throated. Nobody worried about the neighbours. If the language was a bit free, well, they were free-and-easy people; if there was a tremendous amount of leg-pulling and not a little horse-play, there was no salacity and no 'dirt'. The parties went on until the small hours, but there was little drunkenness. It was not good manners to get drunk at a party. And also, they could 'carry their corn'.

Mr. Percy Courtney would be quite tired when it was over. His position was, in that curious Romany slang, 'Ohmi of the Casa'—lost! He did not have much home life, one fears—if that was what he wanted. For there were none of those quiet domestic evenings when husband and wife can talk and plan the future, or indulge in gentle confidences. Marie worked at night and rested some part of the day, or went round getting clothes and sometimes playing matinées. If Percy Courtney went to a race meeting, which was far more part of his life than the Music Hall, maybe she would go with him, but she must not get overtired. Probably he went alone. If he did not go down to the Halls with her at night, he could either sit alone at home or go to a club or the pubs

to see his pals. In marriages such as those, when one
partner is in the most exacting profession in the
world and the other has time on his hands, something
has to give way. The matter is more acute when the
working partner is a star, for the great ones of the
profession, whether stage or Music Hall, have little
leisure and are seldom alone. So, if the less important
section of the partnership cannot subdue his or her
tastes to the requirements of the senior, something
must break and there will be considerable unhappi-
ness. There is no doubt that her first married life
afforded Marie a good deal of happiness. It gave her
a home, which she could have had without it. It gave
her a husband and the status of a married woman,
and it gave her the baby daughter whom she loved.
That was its high spot.

But mixed marriages seldom work out, whether of
colour, race or calling, and particularly when the
calling is theatrical. There is more chance in what the
Music Hall performers called the 'legitimate theatre'
if the acting half plays in town or very infrequently is
on tour. It works out often when both halves of the
marriage partnership are in 'the business', and it
works out very well when they play together. Of that
there are scores of instances. It works out when
callings differ, with more chance of success when the
husband is the star than the wife. For any woman is
fonder of a house than a man is, and a woman can
get much solace out of running her own little
domestic kingdom. Men seldom care much about the
way in which their houses are run, if they have the
handling of it themselves.

So it is very probable that the first marriage was not rewarding to either the bride or the bridegroom. Such things need deep and abiding love to keep them together. Marie was only seventeen when she got married—not an age when one expects mature constancy. Of the inner feelings of Percy Courtney there is no trace. Probably neither of them loved the other enough to ensure anything like permanency. But whatever else Mr. Courtney did not get during his life with Marie Lloyd, he got conjugal faithfulness. She had her own views on that subject. Nobody will attempt to describe her as a saint, or even as a too scrupulously moral woman, but there was nothing promiscuous about her.

V

THE SONGS BEGIN

WHEN the story of a Music Hall star is attempted, a great portion of it is bound up in the songs. By their songs the stars made their impact, and by their songs they are largely remembered, and it is certainly by that means that their personality can be caught by generations which knew them not. In that point, and in that point only, they have a slight advantage over the star of the theatre. The performances of players in great roles are remembered by those who saw them, but cannot really be sensed by those who did not and by successive generations, who can only read of their art and never know it. The film star is the luckiest of all; his or her acting is preserved for posterity, and it is most interesting to watch old pictures and see how talent developed, grew, and blossomed. To see Chaplin in an early 'short' and then see him in one of his latest films, *Limelight*, or another, is to have biography of art brought to life. But generations who never knew Marie Lloyd and who cannot see her imprinted on celluloid, can still form a pretty good picture when they hear her songs.

For those Music Hall songs were individual, written *for* the performers, and sometimes *by* them. The personality survives. You have only to hear one of Florrie Forde's songs or Victoria Monks' to get a picture of the robust singer, and Kate Carney's

massive Cockney 'Arriet is fully enshrined. Harry
Lauder lives before you, and so does the genial,
good-natured speed of Harry Champion. Gus Elen's
somewhat saturnine coster is well displayed, and so
is the more glamorized version of Albert Chevalier.
Mark Sheridan, Whit Cunliffe, and Charles Whittle
live on in their remarks about the seaside or the
desirability of going down the Strand. Dan Leno is
more remote, for he was greatest in his patter, but
his gigantic partner, Herbert Campbell, looms as
large as life, as does George Lashwood's robust
method. When you hear, *I Stopped—I Looked—I
Listened* or *Say No More About It,* Robey and his
eyebrows come to life. That curious elusive charm
which was Eugene Stratton is there in those immortal
songs of Leslie Stuart which, beautiful as they were,
and are, owed so much to the singer. The list could
be extended indefinitely.

Those songs of Marie Lloyd's which have endured
have melody, lilt, impertinence and Cockney cheekiness, and they have some of the radiance too. They
move as she moved, and they are as neat and chic as
she was when she sang them. Of course she had many
songs which are forgotten and many which were
never even published, but enough remain, not only to
make a musical portrait of her, but mark her progress
and recall her to vivid life.

As stated, she began by singing other people's
songs, and then she got her own. The great ones did
not come at once, although many that she had in her
very early days were tremendously popular at the
time and are well remembered by those who heard

her sing them. Sometimes, with the Music Hall performer, the song had much to do with the initial success and the songs did much to make them. But in Marie's case, it was she who made the songs. They were good songs, but it was because Marie Lloyd sang them that they lived and that they still live. In the hands of a lesser artist they would not have made the same impact. Often those songs popularized by Music Hall performers were the big featured songs in the annual pantomimes. They were excellently sung by performers other than those who created them. That was not true of Marie Lloyd's songs. You had to be Marie to sing them, to get the real essence, the essential spicy juice out of them. It was Marie who mattered.

She had some good songs too. And there was one which may give a clue to the reason for the fixed tradition that she was 'blue'. It was called, *What's that for, eh?* Yet the inquiries were of the utmost simplicity, about domestic objects or anything you might see in the daily round. But she, an inquisitive child, wanted to know, and her parents either fobbed her off or couldn't be bothered, in the way of parents of all ages. She sang:

What's that for, eh? Oh, tell me, Ma,
If you won't tell me, I'll ask Pa,
But Ma said, 'Oh, it's nothing, hold your row,'
Well, I've asked Johnny Jones, see? So I know
    now. . . .

Bereft of its very simple context, that speaks

volumes for the reputation she gained, to which must be added the wink, that wonderful wink, and that sudden, dazzling smile, and the nod of the head . . . but there was nothing in the song itself which would render it liable to censorship. The bite lay in what the public of that day called the 'dooble entender', and what their own minds made of it, too.

Marie did not mind very much if they considered her 'blue' or not. She knew what she was about— she was being herself, and by that simple process she was capturing the hearts of a vast audience because they preferred people who were natural to those who were obviously 'putting on an act'. She gave them the choice; they could either take the words at face value or they could take her own face and her expressive hands and eyes, which accompanied those songs as closely as the orchestra the score. If they chose to think the worst, well, bless them, it's their own choice. There was one song, however, which did not require any great stretch of imagination to think the worst about. It was called *She'd Never Had Her Ticket Punched Before*. It was about a poor simple country girl who came up to London by train. She had never travelled in a train before and she did not understand the rules and regulations. She had a most riotous time finding out, because, you see, she'd never had her ticket punched before.

But perhaps the first of her songs which had the distinction of being whistled and sung all over the place, and that was the hallmark in pre-B.B.C. days, was, *Oh, Jeremiah, Don't You Go To Sea*. That song, with a swinging tune and in which she used the full battery of her wiles, really 'got' the public. And it was soon followed by others which rapidly became 'chorus' songs, known to all and sung by all, *The Wrong Man, Never Let a Chance Go By,* and *That Was Before My Time.* Chance plays a big part in theatrical affairs and even more on the vaudeville stage, when Music Hall itself was top of the bill. A chance line in a newspaper produced the immortal, *We Don't Want To Fight, But, By Jingo, If We Do,* and a chance remark at a party gave Marie Lloyd one of her big early successes. It so happened that George le Brunn, who wrote many songs for her, and everybody else, was at that party. In casual conversation, somebody said, in answer to a question about what was to be done in an embarrassing situation, *Oh, You Wink The Other Eye.* Le Brunn heard this and it set his quick and vivid imagination to work. In no time, he had the song written for Marie, and it was an enormous success. It paved the way for another big winner, too, which is probably well remembered by many people today and which gave Marie the best of chances for sauciness and spice— *Twiggy Vous.* Written by Richard Morton and composed by George le Brunn, there was not much that was 'blue' about the song, which consisted partly of advice and partly of comments upon things in everyday life. To read the lyric would not bring a blush to the cheek of the Victorian young person who was so closely protected in those days.

Twiggy Vous started by Marie telling her audience that if you are giving advice or telling a story, it is best not to tell the end, or the point, but to let people guess it, any way they liked. It was, incidentally, her own roadway to success. She instanced certain things: a young husband's rush for the midwife; a young lady climbing on top of a bus in a gale of wind which blew her skirts rather high; a father interrupting a young couple kissing and hugging at a gate; a needy gentleman pawning his watch; and finally an old spinster sighing at the sight of an engaged young couple.

> *Twiggy vous, my boys, twiggy vous?*
> *Well, of course, it stands to reason that you do.*
> *All the force and meaning in it*
> *You can 'tumble' in a minute,*
> *Twiggy vous, my boys, twiggy vous?*

That was a 'blue' song in Victorian days. Times have changed!

That song was not only very popular all over this country, but it spread abroad. One night, when Marie was appearing at the Oxford, a man came to the stage door, asked to see her, and handed in a foreign-looking visiting-card bearing an unmistakably foreign name. Now, Marie's lavish generosity was already giving her friends anxiety, and not the least of them Mr. Percy Courtney, so he and they, very rightly, formed a sort of bodyguard to protect her from stray callers who would, they were sure, most likely beg for help in money form. People they knew could be let in; strangers must be dealt with. This was a stranger, and a foreigner at that, so he was doubly suspect. A most determined attempt was made to get

him to go away: he was obstructed, he was refused
admission, he was even threatened with violence.
With smiling persistence, he kept on asking, most
politely, for the honour of a moment's conversation
with the so brilliant Mees Lloyd. And, in the middle
of the fracas, the 'so brilliant Mees Lloyd' appeared
herself. She took one look, and she told the foreign
gentleman to follow her into her dressing-room. He
did so. And her judgment was right. He was a most
important personage indeed, no less than a member
of the French Government itself. He had come to
pay his respects to a great artiste and to her song,
which, he informed her, was most popular in Paris.
The song was *Twiggy Vous*. Marie was delighted;
champagne was opened and an early *entente cordiale*
was soon in progress. So evidently the Parisians
understood the Anglo-Lloydian French phrase
Twiggy vous. . . .

But there was no French in *Garn Away*, which was
real Cockney, and how they loved it, not only the
Cockneys of London, but the real down-to-earth folk
of every city in the land. And not only they, but the
stratum of society known as 'the upper classes'.
Ladies, of course, real ladies in the Victorian-
Edwardian sense of the word, never saw Marie Lloyd
unless she appeared in pantomime. Pantomime was
always respectable, especially when it was at Drury
Lane, but somehow those songs got into the drawing-
rooms. The writer can remember how, in his youth,
he actually heard a lady of the most unimpeachable
respectability sing *Twiggy Vous* at a musical evening
at a drawing-room of a typical Victorian home and

get much applause. He remembers now, from experience gained afterwards, that she did not sing it in a
manner that resembled Miss Marie Lloyd's, although
maybe she thought she did. But she got much
applause because it was a good song. It goes to show
that, for the greater part, the words of Marie's songs
were innocent.

The audience that particularly adored her—those
of the East End—did not always appreciate this
'blueness' of reputation which the audiences at the
West End Halls so much admired. She was booked
for the Paragon, in the Mile End Road. She had
never appeared there before. She asked old Chance
Newton, the great theatrical journalist, playwright,
and ex-actor, 'Carados' of *The Referee,* that much-
read Sunday paper on the yellowish paper, exactly
how to treat its audience. She was of the opinion that
she ought to lay it on pretty thick. They would
expect it of her, and she was sure that if the West
End liked its sauciness served up in a dainty way,
the East End Music Hall audiences would like it cut
in the way they preferred their bread and butter.
Newton, who knew all there was to know about the
theatre, told her he was surprised at her. 'You, a
native of Hoxton, asking me how to treat an East
End audience, Marie?' he said. 'I don't know what
the world is coming to. You, one of the most popular
turns on the Halls, asking me how to do your business; me, a working journalist? But I will tell you
this. If you really try to be dirty down there—I am
not suggesting that you will be that—but if you try
to broaden your style and make suggestion into

reality, they will hoot you off the stage.' She laughed at him. She said she had never heard such nonsense. 'All right,' he said. 'You know best. Why ask me?'

But he went down to see her play for the first time at the Paragon. He got there a little late and she was just finishing her first song. There was pandemonium. She had used her own judgment. She had laid it on a bit too thick, and they just would not have it. She was almost broken-hearted and in tears. But it was not in her to accept defeat. Artistically, her judgment had been at fault—a thing which seldom happened. She faced them again and sang another song. She sang it in her own way, and made it the character sketch—the way, indeed, in which she treated all her songs in reality. The charm, the cleverness, the artistry and the radiance turned defeat into victory. At once she was accepted as a Paragon favourite. That was what they wanted. They considered they had been insulted by being regarded as 'low'. Their tastes were not low. Marie was not the only one who thought at first that you must lower the standards of decency when playing in the East End. The standards of decency were much higher there than in the West End, and I think that always has been true.

She had a similar sort of experience, although in reverse, much later on, at the Palace Theatre. This, however, was no fault of hers. It was the first time she had 'worked' the Palace, which had only recently been taken over by the great Charles Morton, the man with the golden touch, the creator of Music Hall. Although an old man and considered too old for work by the management of the Alhambra

Theatre, which he had also rescued from ruin and made successful, he had turned the Palace from a disastrous opera house into the smartest theatre of varieties that London had ever seen. The boxes, stalls, and dress circle were packed with ladies and gentlemen in evening dress. The gleaming broughams with perfectly matched horses drew up outside, driven by a cockaded coachman. A 'tiger', or footman, would leap down and open the door. Out came ladies in wonderful evening gowns, glimmering with jewels, and escorted by gentlemen in top hats, white ties, and tails. You see, this was not a Music Hall, but a theatre of varieties. It was part of Morton's genius. He had invented Music Hall by creating a place to which decent working people could bring their wives at a cost they could afford. He knew the value of pleasing the women. Now he went to the other extreme and made everything so smart and so glittering that there was no doubt of the respectability, and so ladies could come to the Palace, a thing they would not have dreamed of in respect of other Music Halls. In the small promenade at the back were the *jeunesse dorée* of the town, dropping in for a turn or two. Champagne was the drink, cigars the smoke; and everything was very high-class indeed. But with this luxurious atmosphere there was, of course, no room for the simple loud-voiced and unforced friendliness of the 'Halls'. Choruses were definitely *not* sung, and applause, if genuine, was 'polite' and restrained.

Marie Lloyd had to face this audience at the Palace—a unique audience—for the first time. She did two of her best numbers, which had 'brought down the house' at the Halls she had already played that night. There was hardly any response, just a spatter of applause, and that mostly from upstairs, where the more ordinary folk sat, in the amphitheatre and the gallery. She was hurt and she was furious. She had three 'numbers' to work. As she changed a hat and few bits and pieces in the wings, the stage manager said to her, 'A tough lot, aren't they, Marie?' She looked at him: 'I'll beat the . . .' she replied. With eyes aflame and with the light of battle in them, she summoned up her reserve and her artistic might. She went on most demurely, almost shyly. She was a small girl, a younger sister of the house, well bred, demure, and oh, so simple and ladylike. The orchestra played the music for the song. It was music that even that audience knew because this song of Marie's had been set to a popular piece of music, as was often the case. This very pretty air was well known, for it was extremely popular with banjoists, and the banjo was a very 'smart' instrument at that time. The tune was *Narcissus*, and it captured the attention of the audience. It was not what they had expected. The law of contrast, a basic law of entertainment, was working. Then Marie sang, with such simplicity, such perfection of characterization, such wide-eyed wondering innocence, as the little girl whose sister was being courted by a young man, and in which operation she was, as a loving sister, most interested. But somehow they didn't want her. Strange as it may seem, she was in the way. She told the audience about it, and slow light of intelligence was dawning. . . .

There they are, the two of them on their own,
There they are, alone, alone, alone . . .
They gave me half a crown
To run away and play,
But . . . umti-iddity, umti-iddity, umti-iddity
aye. . . .

It did the trick. That stiff, starchy audience unbent. They not only applauded, but they cheered. The ladies beat their white kid-gloves together, the men went red with delight and got their starched shirt-fronts crumpled. And, as a final triumph—they even joined in. Marie went off triumphant, to be recalled time and again—or as often as programme time, so strict in a Music Hall, would allow. She had indeed 'shown the . . .' And from then on she was as great a favourite at the Palace as elsewhere.

That story is not in strict chronology, but strict chronology is not an essential of this book, which is designed to show what one of the greatest artistes our country ever produced was *really* like and to indicate how she worked her magic. There is, indeed, no magic in the words of the song. There was magic in the way Marie sang them.

Life was going on much the same for her: almost ceaseless work, 'dates' not only in town, but all over the country; lunch and supper at Romano's in the Strand, the unofficial Bohemian club of London, where she had her own table near the door from which she could see all comers and be seen by them,

too. Visits to the races, lots of fun, plenty of champagne, and maybe a glass of brandy and soda at
times, between the 'houses', to stiffen her for the
ceaseless rush of her profession. Money pouring in
and pouring out again in good living and wild
generosity. There was pride in her house, which was
as spotless as herself, and great pride and love in her
baby daughter, who was the apple of her eye. Little
Marie was growing, but big Marie had grown up.
She was no longer the girl in her teens, surprised at
her success and surprised at the world and what it
contained. She now knew her way about; she was a
woman of the world in which she lived. And everywhere she was beloved. But perhaps she had no
great romance of her own, no object on which she
could lavish her womanly and perfectly natural
feelings with that same generosity as she bestowed
her largesse. It is quite certain that the first romantic
touch which had brought her and Percy Courtney
together had worn thin. There was, as has been
shown, little or no home life for husband and wife. It
was a succession of 'dates' and 'parties'. It irked Mr.
Courtney.

Things had not gone the way he expected. Nor had
they gone the way Marie expected either. Perhaps it
was nobody's fault. They were not a well-suited
couple in any way. She loved gaiety, she loved
laughter. She liked good fellowship and the masterly
masculine of her own type. That would be her proper
mate. Somebody who was, as a man, much the same
as she was as a woman. And a friendship had been
growing. At those parties she met a fine-looking man

who was also a performer. He sang coster songs and was himself typical of the London of which she herself was part. She began to look out for him at parties, to welcome him eagerly to her own. She was delighted when they were on the same bill, and they would make that long and weary Sunday train journey together between 'dates'. It is not likely they would make this alone; there would always be somebody else, for Music Hall folk, if aloof from ordinary life, were, and still are, gregarious. They like to go about in crowds, to play cards with much noise, laughter and argument, to crack gags, to indulge in unlimited leg-pulling. The comics feel that, on the stage or off, they are always working. They can never be at rest; they must always be 'getting a laugh'. If this can be extracted from their companions, all to the good, and those companions were a splendid audience when the comics chose to give an extra and unrehearsed turn during one of the many waits on those cross-country Sunday journeys, at Crewe, Derby, or other big junctions. These places were extraordinarily interesting on Sundays to the observer of theatrical affairs, when this country had so many provincial theatres and Music Halls and when the professionals travelled. 'Legit' companies were conducted by their manager, and one of his most important duties was to 'arrange the journey', although the advance agent usually did it for him. Railway companies competed for the traffic and gave special facilities. A large company could get a special train, but everyone got reserved carriages, and specially printed window-labels made it clear who they were.

There were reunions and happy gossip on those stations at the junctions. But the Music Hall folk were not so lucky.

The 'legits' travelled at the expense of their managements, at three-quarter fares. The Music Hall folk had to pay their own fares and at full price. So often they would come to an arrangement with the touring company in the town. If the journeys happened to be identical and now and again they were, they would arrange to travel with the touring companies and get the benefit of a reduced rate. The 'legits' were always happy to oblige. Of course, it did not always work out for the tours of the theatrical companies were carefully 'booked' so as to prevent too long a journey. The Music Hall performer often had to travel from Glasgow to Plymouth on a Sunday. And even in the days of private ownership and extreme efficiency, Sunday journeys were long and dreary. So, if by luck, some of the 'current bill' had the same 'date' next week, that was a great help and gave company. Now and again, it worked in the case of Marie and the young man in whom she was certainly getting interested. He would always be good company and always full of life and, of course, he spoke the same language. He was a comedian but not a 'low comedian'. He was no red-nosed knockabout, going in for slapstick and 'bellylaughs' but he was a specialist. His line was Cockney comedy. He was the embodiment of the male Cockney, alert, virile, quick witted, rather loud voiced, self-assertive but never aggressive, quite self-confident and with nothing in the way of what are now known as 'repressions' or 'inhibitions'. He was clean, as the true Cockney is; and he was always neat and spick and span. He was a first-rate singer of Cockney songs and his name was Alec Hurley. To all appearances, he should have been the real mate for that embodiment of the women of London, Marie Lloyd. And certain it is that of all the men in her life she really loved Alec Hurley.

VI

MARIE OF OLD DRURY

THE year 1891 was an important milestone in the life and career of Marie Lloyd. In that year she became Principal Girl at the Theatre Royal, Drury Lane, in pantomime—the pantomime of Old Drury, famous all over the world. There is often a misconception about this and a belief that she was Principal Boy there. She was Principal Boy in other pantomimes but never at Drury Lane. For the genius who 'cast' her for the part knew better than that. Marie was essentially feminine and he wanted feminine allure in the often colourless and secondary role of 'Principal Girl'. So he went to the most feminine person he could find—Marie Lloyd.

This man dealt in stars and his pantomime casts were a galaxy. His name was Augustus Harris and he later became Sir Augustus Harris. Everyone called him Gus. He had taken over Drury Lane when it was at a low ebb with a 'To Let' board displayed outside it. At that time he had only £4 15s. 0d. of his own but unlimited ideas and a mind of theatrical genius. He borrowed money and even then, when he started as manager of Drury Lane, he had a capital of only £2,750 in all. It was about enough to pay for one big scene in a modern production. But he was a showman and he had a clear-cut plan. He succeeded beyond the wildest notion of what a man could do. And he was only twenty-seven years of age at the time.

His view was that a theatre prospers under a policy and how right he was! His policy was massive melodrama and prodigious pantomime. A small man himself, he thought and acted in the biggest possible manner. He was a practical man who knew every detail of his job. His pantomimes have become legendary. And he made them startling, so amazing that people were *compelled* to go. One of the things he did was to import into pantomime the great stars of Music Hall. He knew he was right. He knew these great individualists were magnificent performers and he knew how to get them to work as a team. He knew they would draw their own followers to see them in pantomime and he knew that masses of people who would never have set foot in a Music Hall would nevertheless go to Drury Lane to see these amazing people of whom they had heard so much, in the completely respectable surroundings and atmosphere of the great Theatre Royal. And he was dead right; he nearly always was. He formed that combination of comedy consisting of Dan Leno and Herbert Campbell, the most perfect thing of its kind that has ever been seen. He put the Music Hall folk into his wonderful shows and by his genius he made them work as a team whilst still retaining all their individuality. He would watch the Halls and choose his people.

In 1891 he decided that the time had come when Marie Lloyd should receive the honour of appearing at Drury Lane. So he laid his plans. Marie was not impressed, or seemed not to be. Perhaps she played 'hard to get'. Satisfied as she was with her own unassailable position on the Halls, securely

entrenched at the top of the bill, put there not by
managerial wiles or blatant publicity but by her own
talent and the public demand, she gave the impression that as far as Drury Lane was concerned she
was not concerned. This astounded Gus Harris, for
to him, and very rightly, Drury Lane was at one and
the same time the centre and the crown of the world.
His own nickname was 'Druriolanus', bestowed upon
him by that same Chance Newton of whom mention
has already been made, and who had a gift for
inventing such titles and for 'portmanteau' words
affecting 'The Profession'. Journalism then was very
different from today; the writers got space and lots of
it. They could expand as they expounded.

When Gus made the offer to Marie Lloyd, he was
astounded that she did not come running round to
sign her contract and he went after her. She made
an appointment to see him at lunch at Romano's in
the Strand. And there they met, the Top of the Bill
and the Top of the World of the Theatre. They met
at that unique place, the very essence of Bohemia of
the Victorian-Edwardian period and they had lunch
together. Then Gus, with the air of an emperor in-
forming a humble but deserving subject that he was
going to bestow an honour upon her, informed her
that he had selected her as Principal Girl for the
Drury Lane Pantomime at Christmas.

Marie did not appear to understand. 'What theatre
did you say?' she inquired, innocently.

Gus stared at her. 'Drury Lane,' he said, loudly
and clearly.

'Oh,' said Marie, 'but you know, I have played

several dates lately at the Middlesex in Drury Lane. That's what you mean, I suppose. Do you want me to go back there so soon? Is it wise?'

Gus fell back in his chair, open mouthed. He stared at the face opposite him which met his gaze with simple directness and wide open, very blue, innocent eyes. He managed to keep his temper.

He explained about Drury Lane, and the Theatre Royal, the greatest in the world, the place of magnificence and splendour, the first Theatre Royal the world had ever known. He mentioned that it was absurd to think she didn't know it. Everybody knew that palace of drama which had its own guard, like the Bank of England and the Royal palaces. She *must* have seen it, with those sentry boxes outside and the sentries —the guardsmen—in their scarlet and bearskins. . . .

'Oh, yes,' said Marie, a light appearing to dawn upon her. 'Oh, I know what you mean—that great ugly, horrible-looking place at the end of the Lane, with the soldiers outside it. Do you know, I always thought when I drove past it to the Middlesex that it was a barracks or a prison. Still, I'll go there—if you pay me enough.'

Gus Harris was defeated. That anyone could regard Drury Lane in that light: that anyone could so obviously prefer the vulgar old 'Mo', the Middlesex, to the National Theatre, as he regarded Drury Lane, was too much for him. Had it been anyone else but Marie Lloyd, negotiations would have been broken off then and there and forever. But it was Marie Lloyd, and she condescended to come to the barracks, or the prison, for £100 a week. Probably she took less by agreeing to that figure than she would have earned on the Halls. Still, there was no travelling and in her heart she knew it was a big thing for her.

She appeared there for the first time in the pantomime of *Humpty Dumpty* (written by Augustus Harris and Harry Nicholls) at Christmas 1891/2. The cast was: Humpty Dumpty, Little Tich; King Dulcimar, Fanny Leslie; Princess Allfair, Marie Lloyd; King of Hearts, Herbert Campbell; Queen of Hearts, Dan Leno. All tops of the bill and all friends of hers. She was at home. The principal dancer was a girl of great beauty, one of the loveliest women the stage ever knew. Her name was Mabel Love. In all there were over 500 performers. Pantomime was pantomime then! Marie Lloyd lived up to the name of her part and looked lovely and enticing. She sang one of her popular songs, simply dressed in pretty little frock, a pinafore and a sunbonnet. The song was *Whacky, Whacky, Whack*.

She told them she was a schoolgirl and she loved to play with the boys all day, sharing their games at marbles, but she deplored the fact that she and her little brother Jack had to go to school, and if they were late—well, they got *Whacky, Whacky, Whack*....

> *On your tooral-rooral-ido, tooral-looral ay*
> *They whack you half a minute but you feel*
>   *half the day.*
> *I hate those horrid School Boards and so*
>   *does brother Jack;*
> *I tell you straight we get too much of*
>   *Whacky, Whacky, Whack.*

And no doubt every child in the audience agreed with her.

Marie was at Drury Lane for three years in pantomime. Her second, at Christmas 1892/3 was *Little Bo-Peep*. This was a conglomerate sort of pantomime, written by Augustus Harris and J. Wilton Jones. It was a bit of a mix-up but a big success and it introduced all sorts of characters from all sorts of fairy tales and nursery rhymes, as the cast will show: Boy Blue, Ada Blanche (Principal Boy); Red Riding Hood, Marie Lloyd; Bo-Peep, Marie Loftus; Daddy and Goody Thumb, Dan Leno and Herbert Campbell; Hop O' My Thumb, Little Tich; Dame Mary Quite Contrary, Arthur Williams; Rinella, Mabel Love.

The story in the main was that of Red Riding Hood. And in that pantomime Marie nearly ended her pantomime career. She stooped to vulgarity, or what Druriolanus and Drury Lane considered vulgarity, by means of a 'gag'. It happened during the scene when Little Red Riding Hood came to stay with her old grandmother. Gus Harris, with an eye to a little pretty sentimental appeal, decreed that when Marie—Red Riding Hood—was in her pretty little nightie preparing for bed, she should kneel down by the bedside and say her prayers. She did it like a little angel. But a comedian took a hand. Legend has it that Dan Leno made the mischief, but it sounds much more like Herbert Campbell or that imp of mischief, Little Tich. For one night, when watching from the wings at the moment when Marie had finished her prayer, the comedian said, in a loud

whisper, 'Look under the bed, Marie.' Marie was 'on'
at once. She looked under the bed and the audience
roared. She did not leave it at that. Having got her
'laugh' she wandered all round the stage looking for
an article which, in those days at least, was usually
found in a most inconspicuous place—under the bed.
The gag was an enormous success with everybody
but the management. There was an inquest and Gus
Harris was furious. Never before had such indecency
been seen at Drury Lane, well, not since the days of
the Restoration comedies, anyway, and Marie had
never heard of those. The fair, unsullied fame of
Drury Lane pantomime as a 'family' entertainment
had been smirched. It was touch and go whether
Marie was sacked or not. She survived but never did
the gag again. It was not worth the trouble.

She was back again, the next season, too, and again
was warned to watch her step. The pantomime was
Robinson Crusoe, the season 1893/4, and the cast
was: Robinson Crusoe, Ada Blanche; Polly Perkins,
Marie Lloyd; Mrs. Crusoe, Dan Leno; Will Atkins,
Herbert Campbell; Man Friday, Little Tich.

That was Marie's last Drury Lane pantomime and
she was Principal Girl for the third time. Pantomime
was not her best method of expression. She was the
individualist of individualists and the necessity for
teamwork and the portrayal of a continuous
character, small as the demands in that respect were
in the case of pantomime, had a certain restrictive
power on her. Probably she wanted to play Principal
Boy, the centre of interest in all true pantomimes
(though today that position is usurped by the comics,

romance taking second place to comedy). She was to achieve her ambition later, notably so far as the London suburbs were concerned at the Crown Theatre, Peckham. Under the management of its founder, Isaac Cohen, she played 'Dick Whittington' in 1898 and sang a song which was not one of her own, *A Little Bit Off the Top*. It had been made popular by Harry Bedford and was one of the pantomime songs of the year.

Marie got bits off the top which Harry Bedford had never dreamed were there. But she was too definitely of the Halls. She did not belong to any typed style of entertainment. She was her own show, all of it. She did appear in a revue, and in a musical comedy, both of which will be dealt with, but she was Queen of the Halls, so why worry about other things? And she knew she was not such a success in pantomime as in variety. She had always a very true appraisement of her own art. It was no good her friends trying to flatter her about her work. She knew when she was good; she knew when she was—well, not bad, but less good. And not every star had or has that keen self-judgment.

Her advertisement, a whole page in *The Music Hall and Theatre Review* for November 25th, 1895, speaks for itself. It says: 'Miss Marie Lloyd, *THE* London Favourite, has returned to Town after a triumphant Tour of seven months' duration. She will now fulfil a series of engagements at the leading London Halls, extending over two years—Palace, Shaftesbury Avenue, London; Shoreditch; every evening. Brilliant Repertory! Charming Dresses!! A

Unique Personality!!! Christmas, "Dick Whittington", Crown Theatre, Peckham. Agent, George Ware.'

The reference in Marie's advertisement to the charming dresses is worthy of some note. She was interviewed on the subject, and the young lady interviewing her found the great star in the throes of installing herself in a new house. Marie, dressed in a most workmanlike manner, was personally supervising the whole thing, deciding where the pictures and ornaments should go, how the curtains should be hung. She apologized for the disorder and her delay in answering questions, but she need not have done so, the interviewer was getting 'a good story'. Marie informed this lady reporter that all her dresses were made at home—and when there was an expression of astonishment, she said that she herself designed them and that her mother and her auntie made them. 'If I didn't do that, I couldn't have half so many.' And there was a special room upstairs where they were to be made. Indeed, that room was ready and Mrs. Wood was hard at work. Proud mother that she was, she said that Marie herself was clever at dressmaking, which was true. Marie began to display her wardrobe, dress after dress, until the reporter was quite dazzled.

'This is the dress Mother likes best of all,' said Marie, 'and it must be something very special for her to praise it.'

It was a black gauze, short in the waist, low in the neck, with narrow straps for sleeves. It was covered with 'glittering paillettes which flashed and seemed to merge by turns in reflections of every colour imaginable. A piquant, tricornered hat with nodding black plumes surmounted this costume, which was effectively lined with pink.'

'Yes, I like that dress,' assented Mrs. Wood. 'But it wants the limelight to show it off properly.'

There was an Empire dress, with 'the whole of the front of the skirt a mass of exquisite embroidery. A pattern of wild blush roses was carried out in silks, sequins, spangles, and gold and silver threads on a white satin ground, while delicately tinted little shells were interwoven in a marvellous manner. The workmanship was too fine to be properly appreciated on the stage, even from the stalls'. But Marie cared little about that. It was the best possible, and that was what she always gave and what she always wore. Numerous dresses were shown to that young lady from the Press, who was soon quite dazzled and bewildered. There was a pale-blue short-skirted dress with skirt and bodice so thickly powdered with seed pearls as to be quite stiff with them. They had all been sewn on by hand. Another pale-blue costume was smothered in yellow spangles. There was a dress of white glacé silk, trimmed with narrow black velvet rows and chiffon, producing a chic and Parisian effect, heightened by a black-and-white hat with a red rose tucked under the brim. A mauve dress lined with green had a large hat covered with lilac. There was one of deep cornflower-blue, lined with yellow silk and with a spray of blue roses on it. There was one of vivid royal-blue and white and another of lilac and pale green. They all made the reporter most envious, she declared.

Marie showed her the children's and baby frocks she wore for some of her songs. Cut in simple shapes, of blue, pink or white silk, they were bedecked with ruffles, tucks, insertions, and edgings of lace, all fascinating to feminine taste, and male taste too. Marie instinctively knew exactly what she could wear. Her taste for herself was impeccable. She told the reporter that each dress was to have its own separate hook and a large box to hold the hats and other accessories which went with it. Everything would have a place of its own and be in it and easy to find. No costumier could have beaten those clothes made on the premises by her mother, and nobody could have worn them with such effect as Marie.

The house visited in that interview was probably the one in King Henry's Road, Hampstead, to which Marie moved from Lewisham. Shortly afterwards she installed her mother in the Prince's Tavern, in Wardour Street. The mother put a big picture of her famous daughter in the bar, which probably gave rise to the belief that, at some time in her career, Marie was a barmaid. That she never was, although she knew lots about them and sang an excellent song on the subject.

In 1896 she had an offer to visit South Africa, which she accepted. This was her first venture overseas. Her fame had travelled all over the world, but she had not. She decided to take her daughter with her, but relations were strained at that time between her and Percy Courtney, and he objected to the little girl making the trip. This was more than sufficient for Marie, who could never brook opposition. She must have her own way; she had it then. The child was smuggled on board by its Uncle Johnnie. Mrs. Dick Burge, wife of the celebrated boxer and great friend of Marie's, went along as companion, for, like most music hall and theatrical folk, Marie could never bear to be alone.

This venture to South Africa was a great risk. Marie was so essentially English, and the time was just before the Boer War. What delighted London and Great Britain might not please the heterogeneous population of the Cape, the Transvaal, and South Africa in general. But she was a success. She proved then that she was a universal favourite in any country and of any race before which she might appear. They loved the sparkling, smiling, pretty woman in her gorgeous dresses, and with her saucy appeal. They liked those gleaming eyes and teeth, and that wink. And they liked her songs, which included, *Wink The Other Eye*; *Whacky, Whacky, Whack*; *Keep Off The Grass*; *Twiggy Vous*; *There They Are*; *Among My Knick-Knacks*; and *Hello, Hello, Hello*.

By now she was also singing one of the songs she was destined to make immortal—*Oh, Mr. Porter*. Everybody knows that song, or at least the chorus of it, about the girl who asked the porter what she should do, for the railway company had taken her to Birmingham when she wanted to go to Crewe. It will be remembered that she insisted on being returned to London at once, but that she did admit she was a silly girl. But probably very few remember exactly all that happened on that ride. She had been up to London to stop with her old Aunt Brown and had seen all the sights, but the visit had tired her out and she was not sorry to get into the train with her luggage and go home. But, of course, the train was the wrong one. The train was on the move by then and the porter would not stop it. He told her to keep her hair on—a popular catchword of the time—and not to explode. But there was a dear nice old gentleman in the carriage, who gave her good advice and told her to call the guard. She nearly fell out of the carriage, but the old gent caught her leg and pulled her back. She got hysterical, but he soothed her and promised her that if she made a fuss of him he would give her his mansion in London. So she succumbed and promised to be his little wife, although there is no mention of any such proposal in the song. She threatened that if he teased her she would again appeal to the porter to send her home. So everything ended happily. *Oh, Mr. Porter* lives on with its simple but swinging tune, and generation after generation know it and sing it.

It is strange how many Music Hall songs there were about railway trains. Marie had that other one about the girl who had her ticket punched. Wilkie Bard and Will Fyffe were at their best as railway guards, and so was Dan Leno. Even the introduction of ragtime could not take away the romance of steam, nor could the motor or the aeroplane conquer it. When jazz and ragtime arrived, the steam train still held its own— *The Five-Fifteen, The Midnight Choo-Choo* with Alabama as its destination, and even *The Acheson, Topeka, and the Santa Fe*. Will the diesel get the same regard, one wonders?

Whilst in South Africa, Marie gave her little daughter her stage chance. The child was a clever mimic and imitated everyone, including her mother, whom she so greatly resembled; and as Little Maudie Courtney, she was a great success.

*   *   *

South Africa just laid its heart at the dainty feet of Marie Lloyd, and she bathed that land of sunshine and gold in her radiant personality and smile. She made friends everywhere, but she got a taste of snobbishness on the steamer coming home. Her companions of the First Class cold-shouldered her. 'After all, y'know, she is only a Music Hall artiste—and rather—rather—well, y'know.' But the time came for a ship's concert and, naturally, they asked her to perform. They were all over her and explained that it was in the cause of charity. She smiled enigmatically, and said she would. The concert took place and was given to second class and steerage as well. The first-class passengers waited anxiously for the chance of hearing Marie Lloyd without having to undergo the smirch of visiting a low Music Hall. But she did not appear. Asked the reason for non-appearance, she gazed at them wonderingly. 'But I have appeared—four times. Twice in the steerage and twice in the second class. They loved me, bless 'em.' 'Oh, Miss Lloyd,' she was told, 'but this is for the first class.' 'I see,' said Marie, 'but the first-class passengers failed to recognize me, so I'm —— if I'll recognize them.' She won her victory.

VII

THE TURN OF THE CENTURY

WITH the coming of the nineteen-hundreds, when the real Edwardian era dawned and the days and nights of wealth and power were at their peak in this country, Marie Lloyd was riding on the crest of the wave. She had found success, wealth, and popularity. Yet she had not found personal happiness. She had adulation from the multitude such as had hardly ever been given to any public idol. She had money which rolled in like a flood. She had an international reputation. She had a daughter she adored. But that real love and affection which can be the corner-stone of life still evaded her. She did not know it then, but she was never to possess it. Everything else she achieved; complete heart's desire she never reached. It is as well, at this stage of her career, to see what others said of her, all of them her contemporaries.

But first, there was always a question which she had to answer, or somebody had to answer for her. Everybody wanted to know how old she was. That sporting and dramatic journal *The Referee* ran a well-informed 'Answers to Correspondents' column which has never been equalled for knowledge and accuracy. Every single week it gave the answer, because every single week it had hundreds of queries as to the age of Marie Lloyd. It kept that answer in 'type' for years, and always printed it; it just altered the age every year. It is a curious thing about popular favourites that there is always a large section of the public which is quite sure they are either drunkards or drug addicts and a still larger section which is positive that they are much older than they profess. *The Referee* could make no comment on the question of drink or drugs, but every week there appeared the line, 'Miss Marie Lloyd was born on February 12th, 1870'. It became a joke. Marie Lloyd enjoyed it. She came round to *The Referee* offices one day with what she said was a 'combined certificate', which read as follows:

'Combined Certificate, 1908
MISS MARIE LLOYD
Notice to All
Miss Marie Lloyd has only one daughter—and she is not on the stage
In answer to all inquiries—
Marie Lloyd, born February 12th, 1870.
The following are her brothers and sisters and their respective ages:
John Wood (not in the profession), born December 17, 1871.
Alice Lloyd, born October 20, 1873.
Grace Lloyd (not in the profession), born October 13, 1875.
Daisy Wood, born September 15, 1877.
Rosie Lloyd, born June 5, 1879.
Annie Wood (not in the profession), born June 25, 1883.
Sydney Wood, born April 1, 1885.
Maud Wood, born September 25, 1890.

This is final. Will anyone disputing this, kindly
apply at Somerset House?
Wood is the family name, Lloyd stage ditto.'

She issued this because so many people knew for
certain, so they said, that her brothers and sisters
were really her children. And that sort of thing still
goes on today.

It is as well also to discuss, here and now, those
members of her family who were 'in the profession'
and earned some fame. Alice, a very charming
woman and artiste, was a big success. She worked first
with her sister Gracie as a double turn. Then Gracie
married a well-known jockey named George Hyams.

Alice continued on her own. Alice was a first-class
single turn and an excellent Principal Boy. She
married Tom McNaughton in 1905. He was a very
clever comedian, one of the Brothers McNaughton.
Alice was successful in America, where she remained
for years. She came back to England in 1918, and her
husband died in 1923, after a married life of perfect
happiness. She died only a few years ago, charming
to the end.

Daisy kept to the family name and never was
known as Lloyd. She made a big success for herself,
too. She was smaller than her sisters, but very bright
and vivacious and an excellent Principal Boy. She
was a superb dancer, and many may remember her
singing *Down on the Farm* with the speedy, quick,
mercurial dance which followed it. She married, not
a performer, but a man named Donald Munro, who
owned much property and real estate, including the

freehold on certain Music Halls. Daisy Wood retired in her prime. She could, one thinks, have gone on for ever, for she seemed to have perpetual youth.

Rosie began her career with another girl, Bella Orchard. They were billed, in the somewhat familiar way of those times, as 'duettists and dancers'. But they called themselves The Sisters Lloyd. Bella Orchard married Dick Burge, the boxer, and left the stage, and Rosie worked on alone, eventually marrying Will Poluski, Junior, scion of a famous Music Hall family. She excelled as a singer, and had probably the best voice of the whole family. Mrs. Dick Burge—the erstwhile Bella Orchard—was Marie's companion on that trip to South Africa, it will be remembered. Dick Burge had a tragic life, for he became involved in a bank swindle and served a term of imprisonment. It was generally considered that he could have cleared himself if he had 'split' on others, but that he would not do. The public never lost faith in him, nor did his wife, nor any of the Lloyds, who stood by him through thick and thin. When he died, his funeral was attended by thousands, who remembered his fine record in the Ring and chose to forget what the Law had considered his guilt. The rest of the family do not really need a place in this picture of the sister who had to make a public announcement that she was not their mother, to silence gossiping tongues.

H. Chance Newton of *The Referee*, who knew Marie well, refrained, when she died, from writing much about her stage genius. That was known to all. What he concentrated upon was her large-hearted generosity. He saw it at close range during the time she rehearsed and played in a musical comedy which he wrote for her. He says, 'The way in which our ever eccentric little friend and star behaved to the chorus girls and men, the supers, and other so-called "minor" people: the manner in which she unswervingly helped them, secretly arranging for food and refreshments, for cabs, etc., in the small hours of the morning, will never be erased from my memory. Since then, too, and right on to her fatal illness, which robbed the stage of one of its most artistic and most deserving of artistes, Marie never lost, but even made, opportunities to help and succour the needy, the starving and those stricken by death. In fact, Marie was one of the three lady theatrical-cum-variety stars who, not only gave their money lavishly to the poor and the suffering, but who gave (as I well know) active service to such unfortunate folk by clearing up their poor rooms, or watching by their bedsides. . . .'

Arthur Roberts, that amazing comedian and inventor of Spoof, knew her well and had many stories about her—and her downright methods of thought and speech. He recalls how Albert Chevalier made his debut at the London Pavilion, a straight actor who was putting a new method of work to the touch and who was appalled at the noise of the rowdy audience which then frequented the 'Pav.' But he made a big success. And, standing in the wings, was Marie Lloyd, always ready to help, with the words of his songs in her hands, ready to prompt him if nerves made him 'dry up'. She was genuinely delighted at his success, but horrified and surprised when he said, regarding the audience:

'I can't stand it. The horrible din. The awful row they are making. I have never played in such a row in my life.'

Marie, who was already a veteran of the Halls, was astounded. 'Row,' she said. 'Did you say row? Why, tonight they are as quiet as b—— church mice!'

Roberts knew her well. He said she was one of the greatest of them all and that, as she was in her youth, so she was to the end, the most improvidently generous woman he ever knew. 'Throughout her life she had an open heart, and I cannot think of anybody who went to her with an open hand who did not leave the stage door with something to put in his pocket. She used to ask me to wait for her after the "show" to protect her from the sharks who were always hanging about in the wings ready to seize hold of all her earnings. I can see her now. Her little head would waggle like the nodding head of a Chinese mandarin. Always apparently happy through the dark days of those first, second and third disastrous marriages, she would greet everyone with a smile and a gift. I have often seen her in her dressing-room ill and weak, protesting that she could not go on the stage that night. Then, when her turn came, she would go on and sing and act in such a way that made you exclaim, "Why, she has never been so brilliant before in all her life." While she was on the stage, busily earning money for other people, she was the spirit of life and buoyancy. When she

had thrown her last magic smile to the audience, she
would often totter into the wings.'

There is no doubt of how genuine Arthur Roberts
was in all he said of her. He knew all about it himself. He knew how to be improvidently generous and
to want the money badly which he had given away.
but he, too, was a great artist, and in the same line
as Marie Lloyd. He was the Puck of his time, the
Robin Goodfellow of London. Only once, he said,
had he seen Marie really upset. She appeared in
Paris. They made her very welcome, although they
did not understand a word she said. But she had an
artistry which needed no language, which was
universal, and she left the stage to loud shouts of
'*Bis, bis*'. She heard this, and fled to her dressing-
room in floods of tears. 'Take me back to England
at once,' she demanded. 'Take me back where they
love me, away from these hateful people.' 'But
Marie,' said a friend who was with her, but was not
allowed to say more before she burst out again. 'It's
no good,' she sobbed. 'I've done my best, and all they
have called me is "beast".' It took some time to
convince her that 'bis' was French for 'encore'. She
insisted that she had always understood that 'encore'
was a French word—couldn't they speak their own
language, then? . . .

Sir Seymour Hicks summed her up in that succinct
phraseology of his own. 'She was the Lady Bancroft
of the Halls, having that incomparable comedienne's
power of holding an audience silent and then con-
vulsing it with laughter by the movement of an eye-
lid. She was good nature and generosity itself, and

gave to all who asked her with both hands, only regretting, I think, that she hadn't three.'

Perhaps the only other woman of her time on the Music Halls who had the same fascination for her audiences and was held in something of the same affection was Vesta Tilley. But the method was as different as were the women themselves. For Vesta Tilley there was great admiration for her artistry, but she was a male-impersonator, and as such was never so much the absolutely feminine character as was Marie. She could fill any theatre, as Marie could, and she was an idol of idols, too. But there was never the same deep love for her as was felt for Marie. She was never quite the same pal, she was never quite one of themselves. Vesta Tilley had all those things which Marie had—wealth, success, popularity, and very great talent. She had much that Marie never achieved—a happy married life, an ability to keep her money, and to be 'My lady' when her husband, Walter de Frece, was knighted. Yet there was never the same spontaneous affection for Vesta Tilley. She lived a long life, outliving her time. Marie went to her grave escorted by tens of thousands. Marie Lloyd wrote no life-story, but if she had, it is safe to prophesy that she would have made many graceful references to Vesta Tilley, who did write her life-story, and makes just one reference to Marie—'that very great artiste, Marie Lloyd'. Vesta Tilley, male-impersonator, was refined, never even the palest of azure. Marie Lloyd had the gusto of Rabelais. But both were great—very great. Had Marie Lloyd lived today, she would not have been regarded as 'blue', but as rather refined. But she lived in days of more circumspection and convention, and the legend has come down, totally undeserved. Nobody is pretending that she and her work were pure as the undriven snow. But by today's standards, she was barely vulgar. . . .

She had now been singing songs for years which had great vogue. Her bicycle song is a good example. For that, she wore baggy 'bloomers'—considered very naughty indeed (one wonders what effect a Bikini costume would have had—of course, it would have led to arrest), and it coincided with a boom in cycling.

> *The fellows all chi-ike*
> *When they see me on my bike,*
> *But I'm as cool as any icicle*
>   *When a saucy bloke says this,*
>   *'Mary, I should like a kiss,'*
> *I only say, 'Salute my bicycle.'*

That song was about 1896. But they followed one another in quick succession, and their very titles may stir the memories. Some were sung in smart dresses, some in character costumes, some in real coster attire. It was when she dropped into the 'vernacular' that her admirers liked it best. What could please London audiences better than her description of her trip to Paris? She had gone there, it appeared, in the full 'Arriet costumes, the long skirts and lots of petticoats, the velvets and the satins, the huge hats with their enormous feathers—to startle Paris, and Paris had, in turn, slightly startled her. She had not

been able to understand what the lady was singing
in the French Music Hall, and her 'bloke' told her it
was just as well. But, after all, she thought, Paris was
not so bad. . . .

So I'd like to go again
To Paris on the Seine,
For Paris is a proper pantomime,
And if they'd only shift the 'Ackney Road,
And plant it over there . . .
Why, I'd like to live in Paris all the time.

Then would come the roar of approval from, not
only the Londoners, but all the people of Great
Britain. For she was so perfectly sure of the
superiority of her nation over all foreign parts and
foreigners, that they gave her their whole-hearted
support. There she was, smiling at them, with those
bright eyes and gleaming teeth, the very essence of
English womanhood. She could do marvels with
smart clothes, and those who saw her sing *Directoire*
Gown, when the slashed skirt showing the leg came
into vogue, never saw that very difficult style worn
to better advantage. Whatever the costume, she could
wear it to perfection. She made even the unromantic
and unsexy bathing-dresses of the period look full
of allure. She wore one in a song which was, one
thinks, called *Every Little Movement*; today she
would have appeared overdressed even for the street
in summer-time. She had that power of suggestion
without words which was quite amazing. And by
inflection, or a little interjection like 'Eh?'—she
spoke volumes. Sometimes she did not seem to feel

the need of thought at all. Silence and, maybe, thought transference did it and, above all, the appearance of enjoying herself.

Perhaps one of the best which gave her scope for the delineation of Cockney life was *The Coster's Wedding March.* In that she reproduced the exact conditions and doubtless the exact emotions through which so many of her fondest admirers had passed on their wedding day. . . . There they all were in their best clothes, doing it well, with a church service very likely at the celebrated church in Bethnal Green, where they married them in batches at Easter-time. She described the whole thing with amazing gusto and reality to life, and admitted that in their wedding finery they all felt as stiff as starch,

> *But the parson smiled upon us*
> *Said, 'The Lord have mercy on us,'*
>   *Down the aisle we did a trek*
>   *With the rice arahnd our neck,*
>   *And we all did the Wedding March.*

She put so much abandon, so much of the real spirit of London and Hampstead Heath into the song and her version of *The Wedding March,* that it was like a tonic. Her wink when she uttered the parson's plea for mercy spoke volumes for the utterly uninhibited Cockney bride. It was, taken as a whole, a remarkable piece of character acting. You never saw the bridegroom, of course, in his bell bottoms and his pearlies, but she made him mentally visible to you—a rather flustered figure, his cheekiness gone out of him, rather a flustered cock-sparrow before the utterly triumphant bride, who had achieved victory in getting her man and had none of the mock modesty of her more aristocratic or more gently born sisters.

Naomi Jacob, in her excellent and discerning biography *Our Marie*—to which all students of Marie Lloyd must be for ever indebted and the mere existence of which makes it so difficult to write a book about this great artiste—is of the opinion that it was a pity Marie never essayed a Shakespearean role, as one of the Merry Wives of Windsor. What a pair she, as Mistress Ford, and George Robey, as Falstaff, would have made. But better than Mistress Ford would have been Marie's Mistress Quickly or Doll Tearsheet. If a discerning producer had left her alone with those parts—well. . . .

There were so many songs during the earlier part of her career and also during its height. She never worked a song to death, and she was always getting something new. Yet she was nervous when putting a new song over for the first few times. Not for her the brazen confidence of the mediocre talent; she was the true, sensitive artiste. She would be topical, too, as *Directoire Gown* showed, and her *A.B.C. Girl*, when teashops became so very much in demand. How that particular branch of the A.B.C. would have been crowded if Marie had really been a waitress there. There were *Tricky Little Trilby* and *The Bond Street Tea Walk*, which she preferred, she said, to *The Cake Walk*. That was in 1902. And there were those of more general appeal, like *The Barmaid*, in which she gave an exact picture of one of those remarkable women—they do not exist today—who ruled their little kingdom from behind the bar. Who understood their customers and were the confidantes who never betrayed a secret and who gave advice which was indeed often taken and always turned out to be good. Not all the barmaids of that period were the loud-voiced, made-up peroxide-haired sirens they are so fondly believed to be by those who never saw them. They were women of the world who, in their little circle, wielded immense power and had a moral code of their own which was impeccable. They had to listen to all sorts of rubbish and appear to be amused; they had to put up with a lot of things which other women knew nothing about—but by and large they were the mistress of the situation and their influence was good. Marie knew all about them. She understood.

Other and earlier songs belonging to the nineties were *The Rich Girl and the Poor*—a nice piece of contrasted philosophy which never descended to bathos—*Not for Bill, It's a Jolly Fine Game Played Slow, Don't Laugh* (1892), and *The Wrong Girl* (1895).

She handled lorgnettes in one song, probably the 'Directoire' number, in a manner any duchess might have envied. But in the character songs everything was exact. You never saw smart shining high-heeled shoes or silk stockings when she was doing a low-life study; her hat, her fur tippet, her apron, and even the handbag were right to an eighth of an inch, and just the right shade of dinginess or shabbiness. There was no glossiness of newness, no suggestion that this was a stage costume. It was always real and genuine, as she was herself. She knew her job, and she would have either fainted in horror or 'said her piece' as only she could say it, at some of the presentations she might have run across today.

Several songwriters contributed to those songs of hers—from old Joe Tabrar downwards. George Rollitt wrote a very good one, *Eh—What?* which King Edward VII quoted on the famous occasion at the London Coliseum, when the little railway built specially to conduct Royalty from the stage door to the Royal box refused to work the first time it was used. The man who suited her best was George le Brunn, his brother Thomas often writing the words. *Oh, Mr. Porter* was theirs. George le Brunn was also concerned in *The Two Of Them On Their Own, Wink The Other Eye* (the words of that were by W. T. Lytton), and many others.

Her 'billing' on early programmes has interest. At the Tivoli she was 'Miss Marie Lloyd—Comedienne' for a long time, until she suddenly blossomed forth on one as 'Miss Marie Lloyd—Queen of Comediennes'. It bears no date, that particular programme, but was probably the late nineties. On the bill with her were Lily Iris, Lotto, Lillo and Otto, Millie Lindon, James Fawn, Joe Elvin, Peggy Pryde, Tom Costello, Bransby Williams, Alec Hurley, Bessie Bonehill, and T. E. Dunville. There were twenty-one turns in all, and the least of them would be a star today. Prices were from one to five shillings.

At the London Pavilion in 1895 she was billed just as 'Comedienne'. At the Empire in 1892 she was billed as 'serio', and in 1893 as 'serio-comic', whilst the Alhambra announces her by name only or as

'The Popular Serio-Comic'. At the Oxford in 1892 she is 'The Droll, the Oxford favourite'—and at the same hall in 1893 she is 'Comedienne', but in 1894 she is 'The Droll' again, and back again in 1895 she is just 'Comedienne'. It did not matter; she was Marie Lloyd. That 1895 Oxford bill is interesting, for besides Marie it contained Florrie Gallimore, Harry Atkinson, Fred Earle, Albert Christian (who first sang *Soldiers of the Queen*), Lotto, Lillo and Otto (they were trick cyclists), Harry Tate (billed as 'The King of Mimics'), Lieut. Cole (a wonderful ventrilo-quist), R. G. Knowles, Cyrus Dare, The Kellinos, Sybil Arundale, T. E. Dunville, Kate James, Arthur Rigby, and a remarkable sketch of military life (so it said on the bills) called 'Drummed Out', featuring A. C. Lilly. One wonders what would happen to that sketch today. But there were twenty-four turns in all—and you could see them, Marie Lloyd, Comedienne, thrown in, for a shilling.

Marie's only appearance in revue was made at the Tivoli in 1902, in a special show called *The Revue*, written by Charles Raymond and Philip Yorke, lyrics by Roland Carse, and music by Maurice Jacobi. It was the idea of George Gray, the famous sketch comedian. It celebrated the Coronation of King Edward VII. Little Tich and Marie Lloyd, with George Gray, were the stars, and the scenes repre-sented the chimney pots of London by night, a grand Coronation stand in the Strand, courtyard of the House of Commons, and Ludgate Circus—with a tableaux, Great Britain and her Colonies.

VIII

THE SECOND ATTEMPT

MARIE was no angel; she had her moods and her fancies, and was not an easy woman with whom to live, a fact which is true of many artistic people and all geniuses. It seems possible that not even her magnificent success with the public gave her the pleasure it should have done. She was restive at one period because of that label of 'blueness', which was attached to her. She decided that the best thing to be done was to leave the Halls altogether, since apparently they only liked her on account of the suggestive methods she was supposed to trade upon. Marie decided to go into 'legitimate' spheres. She was not happy in her married life and never had been. Now there was a new attraction in the offing. The man who now really did seem to be her affinity, Alec Hurley. For the moment, in her mind, the Halls were played out. She was tired of them and the endless round of songs, the sameness of it all. She would go into a musical play; at any rate, she would try her hand at it.

It was to her old friend Chance Newton that she turned for advice and help. She had a 'backer', and he agreed to pay her a big salary for the period in which she was away from the Halls. Later she had contracts to fulfil. But probably they both thought that if the success of the play was big enough, she

could be 'bought out' of those. Such things had
happened. Much later, Billy Merson was to spend
thousands of his own money in buying himself out
of Music Hall contracts—and very lucrative ones—
so that he could go into a musical comedy as actor-
manager and show the world what he could do.
The venture well nigh ruined him. But his ambition
was fired because of his success in revue and as
Hard-boiled Herman in *Rose Marie*. Marie had
no such experience behind her. But her backer
believed in her triumph, and there is no reason
to believe that she had any doubts herself. She
had never known defeat. The backer advertised
this new departure of Marie's widely. She was, of
course, going to tour it and not start in the West
End. The moment the announcement was made
there was not the slightest difficulty about getting
dates. The backer was a busy man. One thing he
overlooked. He had agreed not only to back the
venture, book the tour, and manage the business, but
also to write the play. That is not an easy job at any
time! And so, as time went on, both Marie and the
managements who had entered into bookings wanted
to know something about the play. But nobody got
a sight of it. Marie went to Chance Newton; he knew
all about plays. He was not only a critic and
columnist, but a successful dramatist himself. At her
request, he tackled the backer, drawing attention to
the serious situation that was arising. The backer
said it would be all right. More time passed and
Marie came back to Chance Newton. She had had
three plays given to her from which to select. 'But,'

she said, 'they all turned out to be blinking Bernhardt plays, all right for Sarah, but no good for Marie.' Still inaction. And then, when Marie was bombarded by provincial managers to know what play she was bringing and things looked ugly, as there would be broken contracts to pay for, the backer came to Chance Newton himself. That hard-working man was rehearsing a burlesque he had written for the Moore and Burgess Minstrels when the backer, almost distraught, burst in upon him and begged his help. He appealed to their old friendship. 'You are the only man who can get me out of this mess,' he pleaded. 'You simply must help me. You must write the play for Marie.'

There was barely a fortnight to spare. 'Carados' enlarged on the difficulties. Nobody could write a play, get a score composed, cast, and rehearse it in a fortnight, he declared firmly. The backer was convinced that there was one man who could do it, and that man was Chance Newton. Marie added her plea, and that did it. He set about his task. George le Brunn composed the score, and there were minor delays on account of that composer's little habit of leaving the lyrics which Newton gave him in various pubs as he came and went to rehearsals. Gustave Chaudoir, the musical director of the Moore and Burgess Minstrels, provided some melodies, too. And, to help speed up things, Newton got some numbers from a young composer fighting for an opening, who insisted on being billed as 'Graban' in the programmes. He was afterwards much better known as Granville Bantock.

Just in time, Marie and her company arrived at the Grand Theatre, Wolverhampton, managed by that experienced man of the theatre, who later became secretary of the Royal General Theatrical Fund, Mr. E. H. Bull. The epic was called *The A.B.C. Girl or Flossie the Frivolous*. Marie was Flossie, and she turned out to be, not a waitress, but a person of consequence. It was an attempt to play a variant of the never-failing Cinderella story. The low comedians in the show, male and female, were W. H. Thomas (famous as Roberts the Broker's Man in George Dance's success *The Lady Slavey*) and Marie Wright (of the famous stage family, which contained Haidee, Huntley, and Fred Wright, and several others). This was a theatrical venture, carried out in the true theatrical manner.

It had a quick ending; there was nothing to stop Marie now from fulfilling her autumn Music Hall dates. All she got out of it was a song—*The A.B.C. Girl*—which she 'worked' for a little time. And so ended the Queen of Comedy's career as an actress.

And what an actress she could have been! The one and only Sarah Bernhardt, for example, once was invited to supper by Sir Henry Irving. With a party of distinguished people, they supped on the stage of the Lyceum, according to the tradition set by Irving. Somebody, who really should have known better, asked the 'divine Sarah' whom she considered the best actress on the English stage, and, like a shot, the great tragedienne replied, 'Marie Lloyd'. You could have cut the silence which ensued. And Bernhardt meant what she said. She did not say it for

effect, or to snub a stupid questioner. These two great
women once met. Marie did an impersonation of
Sarah in the Tivoli revue, and Willie Clarkson, the
costumier, took Bernhardt to see it. The Frenchwoman was delighted. Willie introduced them, and
Marie was thrilled. Sarah sincerely told her to her
face how she enjoyed her talent and gave Marie a
signed photo of herself, asking for one of Marie in
return. Marie had one taken in the make-up she
wore as Bernhardt and sent it along, signed 'Sarah
Bernhardt' and also 'Marie Lloyd'. And Sarah called
her 'the Bernhardt of the Halls'. She went further;
she referred to herself and Marie as 'great artistes'.
She told Arthur Roberts that, of the things in
London, she admired the Tower, the Crystal Palace,
the Houses of Parliament, and the Albert Memorial
—it is hoped that does not shock those who revere
the memory of Bernhardt, but she was of the period,
and she added, 'But you happen to have only one
woman of genius on your stage—and that is Marie
Lloyd. . . .' But even Marie's genius could not make
a success of *The A.B.C. Girl*. It never came to town.
Its script was in the possession of its author up to
the day of his death. Now, in all probability, it is
lost, unlamented. It was Marie's major defeat, but
not her fault. She knew other defeats in private life,
for she never achieved her search for happiness.

Yet, at one time, it seemed so near. She had
separated from her husband, Percy Courtney, and he
went out of her life. Into it came the Coster
Comedian Alec Hurley, of whom mention has already
been made. There is no doubt in the minds of all

who knew her that this was the man she really loved.
They had so much in common. They were of the
same 'profession', both of 'The Halls'. They shared
the same sense of humour and both excelled in the
delineation of Cockney character; Marie excelled in
all she did, but Hurley was purely Cockney. He was
never the equal of the two great stars of that line,
Albert Chevalier and Gus Elen, but he was very good
indeed. He was a good singer and he had personality.
He was not an Adonis, but in the manner of the time
he was attractive. Full of sparkle and life, he loved
laughter and seemed the very mate for Marie. It
seemed that, at last, the happiness she wanted would
come to her as a return for the happiness she gave to
others. What seemed so grand to them was that they
could tour together and share their triumphs and
applause together, and although they would be, of
course, individual 'acts', they would otherwise be in
double harness off-stage, if not on it.

To attain the happiness she felt was in store for
her, Marie was divorced. Percy Courtney obtained
the divorce, and she was regarded as the guilty party.
Much she cared. A divorced woman then was not
'received' socially in genteel circles. But Marie had
no use for genteel circles; she had a circle of her own
and was Queen of it. She would not have been
admitted to the Royal Enclosure at Ascot, but she
did not want to go there. If she wanted to go to
Ascot, she wanted to be with her own pals and have
a jolly good time. Nowadays divorce is less un-
common. Marie was to find, however, some years
later, how rigid was that social bar. But in the

meantime she didn't care two hoots. She could and did marry her Alec, and all seemed a pathway of roses. There was difficulty with Mr. Courtney over the custody of the daughter. He suddenly evinced far greater interest and affection in his offspring than he had shown for years. But that problem was solved, and Marie set off down what she was sure was a sunlit path of love and laughter.

Alec Hurley, on the stage, had a force and direct appeal which came from real true understanding of his art and audiences. He did not have to shout and bellow, as the younger generation think the musical performers were in the habit of doing. He knew his job and did not labour to make his points. He had good songs, and knew how to sing them, a remarkably fine tenor voice of sweetness of tone, which could be gentle or resonant, just as he wished, and he could sing a swinging chorus or turn on the charm and wheedle a bird off a tree. In the best sense of the words, he was a singing comedian. But he was also the embodiment of the London coster—with the independence, the cheekiness, and the complete confidence in himself which is the hallmark of that race, or was then. Such men were not only English, they were London. They spoke with an accent, but it was an English accent, and their City of London was an English city. They dressed in their own way—which owed nothing to fashions from over the sea—but was based upon the tradition of their own race and their own locality. They were quite sure that they and their city were without equal in the world. And they were not far wrong.

Marie could be the ideal Cockney woman—the 'Arriet—but she could also be anything else she wished. But Alec Hurley was the coster, the man from the New Cut, the Old Kent Road, the street markets all over the place, quick-witted, active and resourceful as a London sparrow. You found his type running little shops, landlords of pubs and ale-houses; you found them serving behind bars and counters and serving in the Forces. You found them everywhere in London, but saw them at their best when they had their own 'barrow' or 'barrer' along-side the kerb, filled with various goods—it might be vegetables and greengrocery, it might be fish, it might be almost anything. At night, a naphtha 'flare' lit it, its naked flame blazing away and spluttering in the wind. The 'trouble and strife' in her shawl and jacket or mantle, highly coloured skirt and immense hat—or, if she was mature, it might be a gent's boater in black straw—sat beside the 'barrer' and was the cashier. Her old 'pot and pan' was the salesman. And what salesmen the Cockneys were; they knew everyone, and if they didn't—well, they made it appear as if they did. They had persuasive tongues and could sell anything. They made their customers laugh; all the old customers were their friends. A new customer felt that he or she was a friend also. And he became one. Their own fun they made; they had no radios or T.V. sets. They liked the 'Alls, the pubs, a good old 'ding-dong', Southend for a breath of fresh air, Chingford and Hampstead Heath. They liked their fish and chips, a penn'orth of each went a long way then; they liked whelks, and mussels and cockles and winkles. They had no wish to join the upper classes. They were the Cockneys; that was good enough for them, and they had a kindly contempt for foreigners. They were fond of music and made their own with mouth-organs, which not yet had become harmonicas, and concertinas, which had not become piano-accordions. They adored dancing; the piano-organ was their dance band. They had characteristic dances of their own and were the real natives of London. Their Capital was Lambeth.

Alec Hurley conveyed all that. He expressed his belief in the superiority of all native materials over those imported from abroad when the *Cake Walk*—from America—came into popularity. One of his best songs was called *The Lambeth Walk*. It had nothing to do with the excellent song which came much later from Noël Gay and which swept into vast popularity. Yet, in its way, it was the same as the forerunner. For in that song, Alec Hurley declared:

You may talk about your Cake Walk,
The Lambeth Walk, it knocks 'em all to
*   smithereens,*
It ain't no blooming fake walk,
It's the same as we do when we're out selling
*   greens,*
For we don't want no banjoes, burnt cork or any
*   fake,*
The Lambeth Walk—there ain't no talk,
For that walk takes the cake.

As Alec Hurley sang it, it most certainly did.
Man and wife, he and Marie undertook a tour to

Australia. She was a bit reluctant to go—foreign parts had no call for her; London and her own country—that was good enough. But Alec wanted to go. The offer was a perfectly splendid one; they would be together and have fun. So off they went in 1901 to greet the new century Down Under, beneath the banner of Harry Ricards, a leading Australian manager, who was as English as they, and had started his career as a Music Hall performer, too.

On the boat they had a species of honeymoon, and opened in the Opera House, Melbourne, on May 18th, 1901. Success was instantaneous. They appeared on the same bill, and Hurley sang *The Lambeth Walk*. At the end, a number of 'Arrys and 'Arriets, in their traditional London costumes, did a little dance, the real coster dance, and amplified it with a kind of triumphant strut, full of cheek and confidence which represented the very spirit of Lambeth. Unknown to the audience, on the opening night, one of those 'Arriets was Mrs. Alec Hurley herself, Marie Lloyd, whose own turn had yet to come, thoroughly enjoying the fun of being part of her husband's act.

When Marie's number went up in the frame, there was that same exciting hubbub from the people in the auditorium which it aroused in London. It was different in tone, maybe, for the feeling of personal friendship and real affection was not yet there. These people had never seen, although they had heard of her, and were on tiptoes with curiosity. But they had come to be critical; they scarcely believed that this fabulous woman could be as good as they had been told. They had heard stories about her; they had heard of her naughtiness and her 'blue' songs; they were prepared to be shocked, but they were not prepared to take her at her—or England's—valuation. She had to show them.

The orchestra blared forth her first song, and then, on the stage, full of vitality, full of personality, full of charm, was the small woman with the trim figure, the round face, the shining eyes and teeth, the warm, friendly smile, the perfect command of herself and the situation, and shedding upon them that radiance which was so peculiarly hers. They gave her a thunderous welcome; they could not help it. And she sang to them. The house was at once full of the electricity she always generated. She told them about *The Barmaid*, and they adored the barmaid, and all wanted to go to 'the Rose and Crown'. She told them of the joys of going to Folkestone for the day, and doubtless many of them registered the vow that they must take a trip 'Home'—England was and still is Home to them—and sample Folkestone. If it was only half as good as Marie said, it was just the place for them. She gave them information concerning Milly of Piccadilly. In that song, her genius for understatement, her genius for letting the audience fill in the blanks, while she just indicated with those hands, the winks, the little nods, coughs and pauses, was fully displayed. She told them that, despite all that people said, 'Milly was all right', and they roared their agreement. But what captured them completely and had them yelling with delight was the advice she gave them in the last of the songs which formed the act. It met a response in every heart, and they all knew and loved the essentially British, lively, homely, yet appealing, direct, yet unaggressive woman, a lady who was essentially a product of the place they regarded as 'Home', and who was therefore one of themselves.

They liked what she had to tell them, which was that a little of what they fancied did them good. She always believed in having it if she fancied it, she said, but it must be clearly understood that it must be fancied before being taken. There must be nothing of habit or regulation in this; it must be according to inclination. And then they would find that *A Little Of What You Fancy Does You Good*. She gave them several instances, and ended with a direct tip to wives: she told them that her old man had a roving eye and evinced a desire to go off on his own on holiday. Did she object? Oh, dear, no; that was not the way to deal with males. Let him go, but it must be clearly understood that if that was his little game—well, she was going to do the same, 'cause a little of what *she* fancied did *her* good!

Her success was instantaneous, complete and immense, and it was the same wherever they went. They went all over Australia. Hurley delighted all with *The Lambeth Walk*, *'Arry*, *'Arry*, *'Arry*, and other songs, but it was Marie they wanted. It was her they loved. They had long journeys, but they did not mind that. Both of them were nomads. They liked the Australians, Marie highly approving of their absence of 'side', their plain speech, and their habit of saying what they thought as they thought it. She was that way herself. She never minced matters, nor chose words; her profanity was pretty exhaustive, and in another woman might have shocked, but in her it seemed so naturally a part of her that it did not give offence, save to the terribly refined and genteely squeamish. But Marie did not mix with them. And, as at home, everywhere she went she was Lady Bountiful. It soon got around, and those who wanted anything, genuine or scroungers, soon found out what sort of a woman she was and profited. She became the welcome and honoured guest of the Australian people, who spoke her language with practically the same accent, too.

Marie did not like living in hotels, although sometimes in Australia she had to. She preferred a house, or to take over a whole set of 'digs' and there entertain royally anyone who liked to come. The door was always open, the welcome always warm. The guest did not have to be smart and well dressed; Marie welcomed the shabby and the down-at-heel more gladly than the better-off. She gave them treats. She could for a little while take them out of their sordid and anxious ordinary lives and let them have something of which they had dreamed. Champagne flowed, if they wanted it; if they preferred beer or spirits, they could drink their fill, and eat their fill of the best food. This wasn't so easy in hotels which were apt to impose restrictions of their own.

Once, in an English seaside town, she wanted kippers for lunch. The hotel was a bit 'snooty' about that. Kippers were within its orbit, it was good enough to say, but only at breakfast-time. Marie twinkled at the manager, 'Right, old cock,' she said, 'let's play a little game, you and me, eh? Let's pretend it's breakfast-time and not lunch-time, and 'ave the blinking kippers, eh?' She got them.

Alec Hurley liked the Australians, too, and he liked their love of sport. Like all Cockneys and practically all Music Hall 'ohmès', he was a sportsman. So he and Marie went to all the race meetings and placed their bets, being, one fears, little the better for them. Alec blossomed as an owner. He bought horses and raced them. There was one little mare which he called by his wife's name. She started favourite, but she let her namesake down badly. She never won a race.

It is not to be supposed that it worried the human Marie Lloyd at all, who loved racing and went to all the meetings in Australia as well as at home.

Australia was a triumph. She was there with her husband, under a sun which vied with her own radiance. She was the most popular woman on the continent. People crowded to see her in the street. She started fashions, for she was always beautifully dressed and wore what suited her. She was cheered wherever she went. Money poured in and poured out. The golden progress should have brought her great happiness, but she who held the love and affection of multitudes was never destined to hold the love of any one man. Already the seeds of disaster were being sown. Alec Hurley was being disillusioned. The artiste was at war with the man. He began to realize, maybe subconsciously at first, that this was to be no joint 'top of the bill' affair. He was a star who had married a star—no, not quite right—he was

a star who had married a planet. He was applauded
and he was cheered, but he never got the same result
as she did. The husband was definitely in second
place. People said, 'Oh, Alec Hurley, yes, the chap
who sings coster songs. Very good. He is Marie
Lloyd's husband, isn't he?' That was the slow poison
which was beginning to work. Had they been artistes
of the legitimate stage, it would not have mattered so
much. But they were of the Halls and were individualists. And she was far the more individual of the
two. So the battle of pride began—although on his
part only—for the Music Hall performer puts his art
and standing first, before anything. To him it is life
itself. At least two of the great ones, Mark Sheridan
and T. E. Dunville, when they felt they were slipping
from their altitude, had taken their lives. It did not
come to that with Alec. But he began to realize that
he was 'Mr. Marie Lloyd' first and Alec Hurley
second. To him that was disaster.

IX

THE GREAT DAYS

BACK in England, Marie was naturally top of the bill. Her name filled every hall at which she appeared. She was almost mobbed in the streets; she was always called 'Marie', and that is the great test of affection on the part of the public. When, in the case of a public character, they drop the surname and just use the Christian name, then the person so honoured is indeed top of the bill. It does not happen often. A more recent example was a person very different from Marie Lloyd—but one who was a fervent admirer of hers all the same: Ivor Novello. To everyone he was 'Ivor'. Many great ones never got that accolade of public favour; it is reserved for those who arouse universal affection. Even Charlie Chaplin never quite had it, but it was there to some degree. Nobody ever spoke, or speaks, of 'Chaplin'. It is always Charlie Chaplin. One of the greatest men of modern times, George Bernard Shaw, never aroused one spark of affection in the mass. Nobody ever dreamt of calling him George, or Bernard. A select few might mention 'G.B.', but never the public. Admiration, yes; he inspired that, and respect. But affection? Not a bit. Sportsmen get it. 'Ranji' had his pet diminutive; Steve Donoghue was always 'Steve'; and anyone speaking of Stanley today is understood to mean Stanley Matthews, king of footballers.

Gordon Richards was 'Gordon' until he got knighted;
and W. G. Grace was always 'W.G.' With Marie, it
was just Marie. Everyone knew who was meant.

Yet she was more popular in certain towns than
in others, a fact common to most public favourites.
London looked upon her as its own, but Birmingham
ran it a close second. Sir Edward Moss, the great
Music Hall magnate, had been scared to give Marie
a date in Edinburgh, fearing that she would not
appeal to the somewhat lofty mental attitude of the
city. Edinburgh is, perhaps, the most consciously
'capital city' in the world, with a cultural outlook of
its own, independent of what other lesser places
think. It is, in fact, almost the only place where one
can get a really critical judgment on a new play
or performance which is not in the least influenced
by renown or publicity. It may be a cold and hyper-
critical assessment, but there it is. Glasgow is far
more warm and friendly. It is infinitely more human.
Edinburgh seems to stand on the heights of its Castle
and its attendant hills and view impartially.

Moss feared that Edinburgh might not like this
woman who had nothing to do with heights, but was
right down to earth. But he took the risk and found
he need not have worried. All Edinburgh did not
live in the Georgian splendour of the new town;
Princes Street, magnificent thoroughfare that it is, has
all sorts of passers-by. Auld Reekie threw over its
austerity and took Marie to its heart.

But once, in Sheffield, she had trouble. At the first
house on the Monday she did not go at all well.
She went badly. This was a novel experience, and she

went into a pretty bad fit of temper. On occasion she could storm like a cyclone in the China Seas. Off the stage she rushed, banged into her dressing-room, told all and sundry within hearing, before she slammed the door that she had done with Sheffield, and she gave her opinion of its inhabitants in words as well tempered and cutting as the objects they manufactured. She consigned them all to the condemned depths of the infernal regions with adjectives as lurid as its flames. Enthusiastically, she set those cutlers a task. She told them exactly what they could do with their knives, their scissors, and particularly their circular saws. She announced her intention of not playing any more that week, and the management feared that she would keep her word. On the same bill was Harry Claff, a fine singer, known on the Halls as 'The White Knight', because he played in shining armour. Harry was a popular man, who did great good for his colleagues by his work on the Variety Artistes' Federation—and he had charm and tact. The management asked him to approach Marie and get her into a good mood. Harry, who knew her and how to handle her, tackled the job. He knocked on the door and heard the loud recriminations which still went on within die to silence. Then Marie's voice asked who it was, and he said, 'It's Harry Claff, Marie.' Sharply he was told, 'Come in,' and in he went.

Marie looked at him, lightning in her eyes. 'I know what you've come for, Harry,' she said. 'You've come to schmooze me, to smooth me down. Well, my lad, it can't be done. I've finished with the b——, so get out.'

'Nothing of the kind, Marie,' said the tactful

Harry. 'I haven't come from the management; I've come as a deputation from the inhabitants of Sheffield.'

Marie looked at him suspiciously. 'What do you mean?' she demanded.

'Well, what you said about them, and what you told them to do has gone round the town like lightning. You know how it is. The Press got hold of it, too. So they have sent me as their representative. They apologize. They were wrong. And they want me to tell you that, to show you how contrite they are, they are willing to do exactly what you told them with the knives and scissors, but they do beg to be excused from the circular saws.'

Marie burst out laughing, and Harry knew all would be well. You had only to make her laugh and the storm passed away. She played the second house, and Sheffield acclaimed her. The circular saws remained undisturbed. . . . Naomi Jacob tells that story in her book, and as it was also told to the writer of this one by Harry Claff himself, an old friend, it is used again and is well worth it.

If Marie felt offended, she would always seek revenge. Once she achieved that, all was well. When she moved into the house in King Henry's Road, Hampstead, a bill from an upholsterer, a very large firm indeed, was overlooked. So were the statements, and Marie, who always paid her bills, was apt to be careless on occasions. Instead of sending a representative to see her, who would have got a cheque from her at once, they issued a writ. She took that as a diabolical insult. And so, on the following

Saturday morning, a few minutes before closing-time, the manager was told that Miss Marie Lloyd wanted to see him. He came out all smiles and bade her welcome, asking what he could do for her. His smiles met with no response.

Marie looked like thunder. 'So you are the bloke that's blistered me,' she said. The manager did not quite understand, he said. 'Oh, yes, you do,' said Marie, 'you put a blister on me, bunged me a writ for your potty little account. I don't like that.'

The manager was all apologies—some terrible oversight, he explained, some bad bungling by a sub-ordinate—such a thing should never have occurred, but Marie cut him short. 'I know that,' she said, 'and it was an underling. You're the boss, and you're responsible. I've come here to pay it—in cash—and I want a receipt, too.' She motioned to her chauffeur, who stood behind her, heavily laden with bags. The chauffeur stepped forward. 'Here's the money,' said Marie, 'in cash—in halfpennies. And I want 'em all counted and a full receipt before I budge or before you shut your —— shop. Half-bankrupt, I expect, or you wouldn't go dashing blisters about.' And she had her way. They had to count out those halfpennies and give her a receipt before they dared close the shop. She kept that establishment open over half an hour and told the staff to blame the 'b——, blistering governor' before she left and entered her car in triumph.

Marie had started a brougham very early in her career, but when cars became practical, she bought one. She felt it incumbent to do so; she could not bear to be behind the fashion. The first was a Panhard, a popular make in the early days of motoring. As time went on, she kept abreast of the popular makes, but she never really liked them as much as she did the old brougham, and it is true that in the early days the broughams were more reliable than the cars.

The 1900's were the great days of wealth and security in this country and the great days of the Music Halls. Nobody realized that before the new century was fifteen years old, a great change would come and the world would never be the same again, and least of all, perhaps, the easy-going folk of the Halls. War, to them, was something far away against some savage tribe, the affair of the small professional army, and they glorified that army in their songs, just as they glorified the invincible British Navy, but sometimes they had wars of their own. One broke out in 1906, when the Music Hall artistes went on strike.

It is of no concern now to recall all that led up to it and the rights and the wrongs. But there had for some time been dissatisfaction over forms of contract and rates of pay. Music Hall was booming, and the performers who made the book found themselves getting extremely poor, or so they thought. Matinees crept in, and while they didn't mind one, they found they had to play two and sometimes more, for no extra pay. There were other little pin-pricks as well. The management had its own version; the Music Hall performers had theirs. There were deputations, meetings, deadlocks. The Variety Artistes' Federation, now a powerful and beneficent affair, fought a gallant fight. The smaller artistes stood to lose the most; the more powerful could resist oppression. But the clash came. The performers struck. There were a few blacklegs, but the majority, not noticeably business-like or given to working together as a rule, stood firm. Marie Lloyd was on the side of the strikers. She knew that if she insisted, she could have got her own form of contract. But she was on the side of the under-dog. The musicians were in it, up to the neck, and they and the performers stood together. Suddenly, on January 1st, 1907, managements found they had no artistes to play their halls. They hunted up old-timers, who were glad of the jobs; they gave contracts to those who did not join the strikers.

A famous act of performing animals was one of the chief attractions as strike-breakers. They could not get from hall to hall fast enough, and their trainer said he had no means of finding out the views of his performers. It was a fascinating battle, and it filled the newspapers. The stars, who were losing big salaries, nevertheless gave large donations to the war funds, and nobody gave more generously than Marie. But what the public enjoyed most was being able to hear, see, and speak to their idols who went on picket-duty. Marie became a picket, and when the sparse audience inside the hall heard that she was outside on picket-duty, they rushed out to see. The unfortunate blacklegs played to bare benches. It is said that when Marie was a picket she did her best to persuade another woman, a minor performer, to give up playing that night and to stop being a black-leg. And she did it in her own way. The woman was

Belle Elmore, the victim of Crippen a few years later. She was never much good as a performer, and one of the pickets asked her politely to stay out and help her mates. Marie took a more direct way. 'Go on,' she said. 'Let her go in; let her play. She'll do more to help break the strike by playing than by stopping out.' It sounds true; one can imagine any blackleg running the gauntlet of a picket which contained Marie. Her terse, forceful, and picturesque comments must have made their ears tingle. At last the strike ended, and the performers won. Always Marie helped her own people.

*   *   *

She went to America, with Alec Hurley. The marriage was still in being, although the disintegration had begun. This was no rapturous trip, as had been the one to Australia. Nor was it so certain of success. For Marie was so typically English that nobody could be sure if New York would quite understand her form of genius.

Her sister Alice had been a great success in the States. Alice was very like Marie in looks and manner, but she worked a different way. She was a very big star in America, all over that continent.

But Marie conquered the Americans. They got a great actress putting over comedy sketches with the little stings of suggestiveness portrayed with art and wit; she was a Restoration comedy in human form. They liked her, but she was not so sure whether she liked America. All the while she stressed her nationality. Whilst she was there, the date came up on which it is customary to celebrate the birthday of the British Sovereign; in this case, King Edward VII. Marie did not care if she were in New York or Timbuctoo. She was an English girl—a London girl—and the fact that she was in a foreign country only seemed to make a celebration more necessary. At home, she would not have taken the slightest notice; except, maybe, to have an extra drink or two to wish 'Teddy' luck. But here, New York must be shown. So in the Astor Hotel she gave a party, and every English artiste in New York was invited. The tablecloth was the Union Jack, and the decorations were red, white, and blue. The stately Astor was startled to hear the band she had hired play *God Save the King* and English voices, her own in the lead, singing that national anthem of theirs at the very topmost power of their lungs. She showed New York what being British meant to her.

Marie had been to America twice before, in her early days, and for very short visits, once in 1889 and once in 1894. But this time Americans saw her in her prime, and she was victorious. Especially the people of her own profession were won, for the night before she left New York when she was playing at the Colonial Music Hall, at the end of the performance Mr. Percy Williams, on behalf of her American colleagues, made her a presentation on which was engraved: 'To Marie Lloyd, the greatest artiste and best friend that we have ever known.'

*   *   *

Again she went to Paris and conquered. She went

to Berlin—where the British were not popular, where few could possibly have understood her, and she conquered. Like all great artistes, legitimate or variety, she spoke a universal language.

At home in England, she topped the bill and continued to keep her Hampstead home bright and shining. Marie was essentially a town bird, but, like everyone else, she thought it right to spend some time in the country, in the open air, although it is doubtful if the open air and country pursuits made much appeal to her. But there was something fashionable then which could blend town and country, somewhere that made it possible to be in the country, in lovely surroundings, and still give parties and live the Bohemian life. It was a houseboat on the Thames. In her inmost heart she probably knew that her second marriage, which had seemed so ideal, was not working out too well, and she may have thought that a houseboat would restore domesticity. So she had her houseboat—indeed, she had two. She bought them from Vernon Dowsett, the manager of the Tivoli. The reason she bought a pair of them was that she felt she needed one to live in and another to sleep in. The living-boat was called *Sunbeam* and the sleeping-boat *Moonbeam*. They were moored near Staines, within easy reach of town and on a very pretty stretch of the river.

In those more spacious days there were few happier ways of spending summer days than on a houseboat. The river was a popular, but unspoiled, playground. There were steam-launches, it is true, but they were few; there were some called electric-launches, which were fewer still. Most of the river traffic was hand-propelled. The peace of the scene was unbroken by the roar or whine of aeroplanes overhead. The sweetness of the river and air was free of petrol-fumes. Ladies in gay dresses reclined in skiffs or lolled in punts, the motive power of which were men in white flannels. There were brightly coloured parasols and cushions, and there was no hurry, no speed, no noise. To sit on a houseboat and watch the river flow by, surrounded by great baskets of flowers, was a blissful relaxation. And at night, the multi-coloured Chinese lanterns were lit, and they sent rainbow reflections over the dark water and the passing craft, each with its lantern, slid by like so many fireflies; the scene was one that cannot be matched today. There was no radio to assault the ear, and no gramophones to churn out mechanized music. There was the plonk-plonk of a banjo and a voice singing melody. What better setting for a party on a Sunday night, composed of Bohemian Music Hall performers, glad to be rid of the grease-paint, the crowds, and the lights, and the rush for a few pleasant hours to see real moonlight on the river instead of the hard glare of the limelight? And what a delightful party it could be, with the aristocrats of the profession each giving his or her own special act for the occasion. Maybe the general peace was upset, but it gave those people joy. The houseboat gave Marie joy, too. She lived like a queen there, sur-rounded by her court—and, maybe, that did not please Alec Hurley, who again found himself in a secondary role. But the laughter, the song, and the wine made the nights gay, and in the morning there was a plunge in the cool river and more laughter.

It is said that Harry Tate's moustache grew from a party on the *Sunbeam*—he dived in and reappeared with a piece of river weed in his mouth, looking like a comic walrus, and made Marie laugh. She suggested the moustache which added so much to that brilliant comedian's appeal. It may be so, indeed, although proof is wanting. But it is certain that Marie encouraged Harry Tate greatly in his earlier days and in his progress from mimic to supreme character comedian. They were friends. Marie could punt, too, and proved adept with the punt-pole. But once she fell in the river and was nearly drowned. Her hat, trimmed with bright-red cherries, showed the searchers where she was. There was one hectic night when the *Moonbeam* sunk at her moorings. Everyone was in bed. Johnnie Wood, her brother, gave the alarm; Alec Hurley, in his pyjamas, was first out and rushing to the rescue. There were no casualties, but all the inmates were caught in their night attire and all their frocks were at the bottom of the river. They had a laugh when they got shelter at a riverside hotel near by, and they salvaged their clothes next day. Marie stopped at the riverside hotel for the rest of that summer, and at the end of the season she sold the houseboats. She had been happy on them whilst it lasted, but nothing which gave her happiness was ever fated to last for long, only her professional success.

The insistent cause of pain in that phase was the

continual accusation of being 'blue'. She never could understand that. To her, the hiding of ordinary life and the little weaknesses of mankind, the 'bits of fun' in which everybody except the Puritans (and she was not so sure about them) indulged were not vulgar or naughty at all. She knew what people talked about at parties, in bars, at the races, and even over their cups of tea. She saw no harm in singing about it. Nor for the matter of that did ninety per cent of her audiences. She was never 'raw'; she was never wilfully dirty or salacious. She would never have cracked the lavatory jokes so common-place today. She clothed the peccadilloes of life with the cellophane of laughter and wit. She was broad at times; she was bawdy, but so was life. So were Shakespeare, Congreve, Wycherley, Dryden, and many, many others. Even today it is a maxim of that most respectable institution, the B.B.C., that if a line implies more than one meaning, believe the least harmful. Marie left it to the choice of her audience. Many of her so-called 'blue' songs would not upset a Sunday school class of modern youngsters. She believed in giving a choice; you could make up your own mind. Anyway, no harm was done if you fancied it a bit naughty, because, as she herself sang, *A Little Of What You Fancy Does You Good.*

She waged war on the straitlaced Puritan brigade who were out to pretend that human nature was a pure, limpid pool and that everybody was a little saint or cherub. She fought them relentlessly—and, with her public behind her, she won. The public never objected. It was a dictatorial minority with no

real understanding of the public mind that caused
the trouble. One recalls that when Mrs. Ormiston
Chant endeavoured to close the Empire promenade,
that she lost the day and attained her only success
by becoming the most popular Guy in the next
November 5th. Although the management of that
famous hall did try to make some slight concessions
to official rulings in the way of a little trellis-work
hung with flowers, these were torn down by some
young men who demanded freedom of thought and
action. At the head of the party was a young gentleman with reddish hair and a determined manner,
who led and helped in the destruction, and then made
his first public speech. He was not arrested nor
punished. He went free to lead his country through
her darkest hour and grimmest struggle to eventual
and complete victory. To day he is the greatest living
Englishman. He would not have disapproved of
Marie Lloyd, or her songs.

But when Marie Lloyd was at her very height of
success, there was a campaign to clean up the Halls.
Indeed, life was to be cleaned up entirely by a body
of gentlemen, excellent in themselves no doubt, filled
with the best of intentions and moral ideas, but with
little knowledge of human nature. Had they possessed
that, they would have known that the British public
can safely look after its own morals, or could in
those days, when the purely British point of view
obtained, and that any performer outraging public
decency would have failed in misery. A powerful
committee was formed to do this cleaning up, and it
had to have its run, because such things as licences

might be imperilled. It acquired pretty wide powers, and, like a Royal Commission, called upon public performers to appear before it and give samples of their work so that judgment could be promulgated.

Amongst those summoned was Marie Lloyd. She was furious at what she considered an insult to herself, her profession, and her public by people who had no right to judge anyone. But she kept her temper. She went along, with a pianist, and she waited her turn. In due course, it came. There was a dangerous gleam in her eye, but outwardly she was all smiles and charm. She sang her song to that committee; all her popular songs, so that they could judge fairly and squarely. She sang them *Oh, Mr. Porter, The Two Of Them On Their Own, A Little Of What You Fancy, Everything in the Garden's Lovely,* and many, many more. She sang them without an inflection, a nod, wink, or smile. The committee was taken aback. This was not what they had expected, and, maybe, not what they had hoped for. If any of them had ever seen her on the Halls, they did not say so. They found nothing wrong. They had a short confabulation amongst themselves, and then the chairman informed Miss Lloyd, with condescension, that she had their permission to continue to sing her songs. She could go. That was the last straw. The fine, healthy temper, so long subdued, flashed out. She was going to get her own back.

'Oh, I can go, can I?' she hissed. 'Thank you for nothing. You've had me here over an hour. I've sung song after song and you've found no fault with them. I can go on singing them, can I? All right. A fat lot you know about anything. A fat lot you know about songs and singers, or what they mean. You've heard those songs of mine you thought so dreadful, and they are all right. Splendid. Now I'll show you. I'll sing you some of the songs your wives sing in your own drawing-room. They are clean enough, aren't they? All right—you just see what you think.'

Marie sang two of the popular ballads which were warbled at pretty well every musical evening at the time, when musical evenings were very popular indeed. They were *Come into the Garden, Maud,* and *Queen of My Heart.* What she did with those songs was nobody's business; the men who wrote them would have been amazed; Alfred, Lord Tennyson would probably have expired of heart failure. Every little word had a meaning of its own, when Marie so willed. Leaving the poor committee stunned and gasping, she wished the members good afternoon and swept out.

It was requesting trouble to cross swords with Marie Lloyd. She nearly always won her battles. She was possessive, too, in her own way, and was proud of being the leading lady of Music Hall. She loved flattery and never made the mistake of believing it. Her sense of character and the fitness of things never forsook her.

Slowly and surely the link that bound her to Alec Hurley was wearing thin. He had caused the break between her and Courtney; not wilfully, but because she fell in love with him and he with her. The deep-seated trouble was that she could not see his point of view. He hated being second fiddle; she never understood. Not that she could have done much about it if she had. It happened naturally. She was Marie Lloyd. He was Alec Hurley, excellent, but not a genius. Had he been content, the marriage might have lasted. But few individualists can be content with less than the whole stage. Had he been a man of strong character, it might have lasted, but he listened to mischief-makers. He ought not to have listened to them, but he did, and the rift widened.

X

THE BAD LUCK STARTS

In the year 1912, the Music Hall profession received the highest honour ever bestowed upon it; indeed, the only honour up to that time. King George V commanded that his subjects who were the professionals of Music Hall should appear before him and Queen Mary at the Palace Theatre on July 1st. This was the first and only real Royal Command Performance concerning the variety profession ever held. All those held subsequently have been merely performances—Royal performances if you like—at which the monarch was present. But the occasion in 1912 was a real command.

The excitement amongst the variety people can be imagined. Who would be chosen? and, equally important, who would be left out? Nothing else was talked about; all other matters were forgotten. Intensely loyal, those people who lived by themselves in their own little community, all desired most ardently to have the honour. It meant everything in the world to them. The pride of the chosen would only be equalled by the chagrin, the complete and utter disappointment—and the raging anger—of those who found themselves not 'on the list'. There is much heart-burning today, when it really matters very little in comparison, and when so many of the artistes who appear are not variety artistes at all. But in 1912—

and for the first time—the excitement can be
imagined.

The task of choosing the artistes was an unenviable
job. The original idea had been the inspiration of
Sir Edward Moss. He had envisaged such an occasion at the Empire, Edinburgh, the performance to
be given whilst Their Majesties were in Scotland
during their annual holiday. But the Empire was
burnt down, and so the idea shifted to London. There
was a good deal of argument as to which Hall should
be selected for the occasion, and the Palace, Shaftesbury Avenue, where a young man named Alfred Butt
(now Sir Alfred Butt, Bart.) held sway, eventually
was chosen.

Naturally, the choice of players could not be made
by one man. A committee was formed, representative
of all branches of the variety profession; a general
committee, which included Sir Edward Moss, Frank
Allen, Walter de Frece, Walter Dickson, Walter
Gibbons, J. L. Graydon, Alfred Moul, Wal Pink,
Oswald Stoll, and Henry Tozer; and an executive
committee, consisting of Alfred Butt, A. Bocchi,
W. H. Clemart, and George Ashton, head of the
famous ticket agency through which the Royal
Family then obtained their tickets and who was
always present in every theatre they visited to receive
them. It was that committee which had the choice.
They pondered, they deliberated; they knew that they
were bound to give offence, to make enemies. But
there were many things to be considered. Even in
1912, just two years before the Old World was blown
to pieces by the guns of 1914, the conventions were

very strong indeed. Nothing vulgar, nothing suggestive, nothing likely to give offence must approach the sensitive ears and eyes of the Royal personages. As Music Hall was primarily a vulgar entertainment, there was an almost overwhelming host of talent which clamoured for the honour of appearing. The feelings of the committee were mixed. The project was discussed, not only by the performers themselves, but by the immense audience, the patrons and lovers of the Halls who had their own favourites and who would feel personal resentment at their non-inclusion. As the Press worked up the story, the public which never went to Music Halls became interested, too. So, for those who were out, there was to be a bitter day indeed. Excitement and anticipation were a-tiptoe.

And then the official announcement was made. It was a long and very well selected list, covering all branches of the business, from acrobats to comedians, from serios to singers and dancers. One great, very great name was not included. Marie Lloyd. It had not been possible, of course, to include anything like the number of deserving people in the main programme, but there had been an excellent idea and 'face-saver'. The last 'turn' was to be variety's garden party, in which no fewer than 150 artistes not otherwise performing would walk on, and thus appear before their King and Queen whilst, as a grand finale, Harry Claff, in his shining armour, would sing the National Anthem, in which they would all join. Marie Lloyd was not even included in the garden party.

The news burst like a bombshell, and had repercussions up and down the country. It was, in fact, a seemingly deliberate insult to the greatest artiste of them all, a woman universally regarded as one of the finest stage geniuses of her time. From the multitude there was a howl of rage. The great mass of her brother and sister artistes resented the exclusion of Marie, too, and felt uneasy about it. The smaller fry were almost ready to hoist the Red Flag and declare a revolution. There was much Press comment.

To Marie herself it was a deep and abiding wound. She had not thought they would do this to her, she, a household word, the embodiment of Music Hall, who knew and was grateful for the love her public bestowed upon her. She had expected she would be allowed to appear. There had, of course, been other omissions—but she was the Queen of the Halls and was barred from its first Royal occasion. She was not considered good enough to walk on in the garden party scene. She was out; she was barred; she was branded; she was disgraced. The reputation had done it; that 'blue' aura was too strong; the whispered stories; the vulgarity and suggestiveness could not be allowed on such an occasion. Of course, it was wrong. She was far too good a woman and far too great an artiste not to have accommodated herself to the special situation. She who could outface a Watch Committee on the sniff for salacity and render them dumb would have given a performance which would have delighted her King and Queen. One is almost certain that her name was on the list submitted to Their Majesties and that some strait-laced court official struck it out. The conventions of the time should be recalled. It should be remembered, too, that at the annual performance the most gracious lady, Queen Mary, refused to look at the stage whilst Vesta Tilley appeared because she wore male attire. And she directed the gaze of the other ladies in the Royal party elsewhere whilst that great artiste held the stage. There was no vestige of scandal to that name—quite the reverse. It was just that she was wearing trousers like a man. So perhaps it is not so surprising that Marie was not commanded to appear.

Marie had plenty to say. She stormed; she raged. She went to see those in authority, demanding an explanation. She would not be appeased; she unleashed her invective on all and sundry; their ears burnt and tingled. Her friends commiserated; those who were jealous expressed their deep sympathy and rubbed salt in the wound. She was not without enemies, but her supporters—and their name was legion—demonstrated in her favour wherever and whenever she appeared. She threw down a gauntlet to authority. On the very same night of the Command Performance and for the very same cause, the Music Hall Charities, she said, she would organize and run an opposition show which would be called 'The Popular Demand Performance', commanded by The People. Marie Lloyd would be at the top of the bill. Very likely she might have done so had not wiser counsels prevailed.

But on the night of July 1st, 1912, whilst a very stiff and stodgy audience sat overawed in the beautifully decorated auditorium of that perfect venue, the Palace, watching the chosen champions of Variety giving performances far below their best, a packed house greeted Marie Lloyd at the London Pavilion, at the other end of Shaftesbury Avenue, cheering her to the echo, demanding song after song, shouting encouragements and assuring her of their love and loyalty. On the bills outside, a special slip was pasted which proclaimed her 'The Queen of Comediennes'. It proclaimed that 'Every Performance given by Marie Lloyd is a Command Performance by order of the British Public'. She had her revenge. From then on, Marie's billing hardly ever varied. She was either 'Queen of Comediennes' or 'Queen of Comedy' And the titles were truthful.

She was having more than her share of ill fortune. She and Hurley drifted and drifted. There were attempts to patch things up, and had he been stronger or she less obstinate, a reconciliation might have been possible. But once Marie embarked on a policy or a line of thought, it was difficult, if not impossible, to advise her. The professional jealousy which divided them was his, she said, and she was not going to climb down. If he broke their marriage, there were others who would love her. Yet in her heart, he was the man she loved most, and there is no doubt that he loved her. They were never together long enough to heal the breach.

Marie was a very restless soul. In her house she never relaxed; there was an almost perpetual party, and when, at unseasonable hours for the profession, nobody was about, she tackled the house itself. She pried into the corners, opened the cupboards, moved the mats, and tested the shelves for dust. She paid no attention to the middle of the room; 'that looks after itself,' she would say. It was the nooks and corners she explored. The woman who had a reputation on the boards for 'dirt', detested it in her home, and did not need it artistically. She was quite sure that Hurley was tired of her, was neglecting her, and preferred other women to her. When they met, they quarrelled; her temper was easily roused, and Alec was not the type of man to still it. He had charm and many good qualities, but not the required strength of will and firmness. It was at a party that the third man came into her life.

Marie loved racing and knew many racing people, jockeys, trainers, owners, bookmakers, and professional backers. They came to her parties; she went to theirs; they met on the race-courses. Two of her sisters were married to men interested in the Turf. It was difficult not to get invited to Marie's parties, and no one invited ever thought of refusing or not turning up. A young man, casually invited in the first place, took to coming regularly and to meeting her on the course, and on other occasions. A quiet, or seemingly quiet, young man, he was a jockey. He was making a name for himself, too; was riding winners, and his services were much in request. But he was quiet and retiring, and Marie scarcely noticed him.

One day he brought an accordion with him. Marie saw it and him, and thought the pair funny. She had a low opinion of the accordion, and the idea that this shy retiring young man should play one seemed ludicrous. His friends told her he played it well, and sang excellently. Marie asked him to play and to sing. The young Irishman sang the sentimental ballads of old Ireland in just the right voice, with just the right touch. He handled that accordion and his voice as skilfully as he handled his horses in the races, and he handled Marie Lloyd just as easily. He entranced her, and soon she saw in him the man who might give her the happiness which she had always sought and never found. She was forty years old. Surely now she knew her own mind—surely now her judgment would be sound. When she married Courtney she had been only a girl. It was on the rebound from her mistake that Hurley had come into her life. Now she was sure she knew. This was a man who was strong; this was a man who did things. He was not a performer as she and Hurley were. Yet he was before the public, and he knew what the cheers of the multitude meant. He was Bernard Dillon, and he heard cheering often as he brought his mounts first past the post. She believed she had found the man who could give her happiness.

Soon people began to couple their names. She was Queen of the Music Halls; he was one of the Kings of the Turf. She would go and see him ride, wearing her best clothes and looking superb. At the sight of him, in the saddle, in his colours, and riding like a centaur, her face would light up and her blue eyes gleam like sapphires. The onlookers could not be in much doubt. And then she made what amounted to a public declaration. She stood right on the rails as Dillon came cantering past, on his way to the starting-post. She called to him, and he reined his horse near to her. She put her face up towards his, and he bent down and kissed it. Thousands saw her look of pride and joy, and they cheered her to the echo. Dillon won. He won the race and he won Marie. Those who backed his mount won their money. But Marie, who backed him with all she had, herself, was a heavy loser. But before she discovered the truth, Bernard Dillon won the Derby on Lemberg for 'Fairie' Cox, and Marie, in the grandstand, cheered herself hoarse. She told everyone that she could not have felt more pride if the horse had been her own. In her heart she believed she owned the jockey.

It was all over with Alec Hurley. Marie did nothing by halves. She was head over heels and madly in love with Bernard Dillon. She was quite sure he was just as crazy about her. She backed her fancy, and it was the worst thing she ever did. Dillon was to bring her pain and suffering, constant bad luck, and hasten her end. There was to be no more joy for poor Marie Lloyd off the stage, and even whilst she was on it, feeding the adoration of her public, the canker was still there.

In 1910, Alec Hurley sued for divorce. He named Bernard Dillon as co-respondent, and he won the case. It brought him little joy and no satisfaction; it started Marie on the path that led to much tribulation. She did not get married to Dillon right away; they lived together as man and wife when there was no bar to marriage. She had moved to Golders Green and was very proud of her new home. Distinguished members of her profession on the 'legitimate' side lived in the district. Maybe she thought she had gone

up in the world. Life went on as usual, and in due
course she recovered from the set-back over the
omission from the Royal Performance. She got sympathy and affection. It is a strange trait in the British
character that the loser is almost always more
popular than the victor. And a man whom they have
beaten themselves can easily become their hero—
Napoleon is the great example—though they never so
enthroned either the Kaiser or Hitler. They make
victories out of defeats, and a pugilist who loses a
championship fight is more likely to be acclaimed
than the winner. So Marie was even more secure.
Forty years of hard work and pretty rackety life had
not dulled her vivacity; had added, indeed, to her
charm and her attraction, and had not dimmed a
trifle of her radiance. She was, as billed, the Queen
of Comediennes. She had a new man and she hoped
for happiness.

In 1913 came an offer for an American tour. Marie
had been there three times before, when much
younger and now she decided to go again, in the
maturity of her power and talent. She knew the tour
would be an ordeal greater than her first appearances
there. The standard of criticism would be higher; she
would have more with which to contend; and that
reputation for 'dirt' and blueness had preceded her.
She did not know how the Americans would take it.
She heard stories of vice and orgies which could not
be matched in her own country. Anyway she accepted
the offer; financially it was uncommonly good and it
would be good for her to be away for a bit; it would
leave her audience 'wanting'. And that is always

desirable. She would come back fresh and be sure of a welcome.

Marie sailed from home in October 1913 on the liner *Olympic* and Bernard Dillon was on the same boat. She thought to slip into America quietly evading reporters who were nothing like so acute then as now, but bad enough. What she wanted most was to see her sister Alice, who would meet her on landing. There never was a more united family than the Lloyds and these two had not met for a long time.

The liner berthed, there was some interviewing and photographing, and the sisters met. But a man was there who was puzzled. A journalist. What bothered him was that Marie Lloyd's name was not in the passenger list. Quite casually he raised the question with her. She fell into the trap. Candidly she told him the truth. The man went and looked again at the list and saw

Dillon Mr. Bernard
Dillon Mrs. . . . and Maid.

London gasped when it read headlines 'Marie Lloyd on Ellis Island'. It was true. The public morality of official America had been outraged. Two people, living in sin, had tried to enter the country. This could not be allowed, if discovered. It was discovered. As the old tag had it, the woman paid. And Marie Lloyd, the one and only Queen of Comedy, the beloved of Britain, was hustled off to the notorious Ellis Island, along with crooks and criminals to await deportation, disgrace and degradation.

Sister Alice, horrified and alarmed, got busy and eventually Marie and Dillon were released on security being found in the sum of £300 each. They did not then enter America but went to Canada and she commenced legal action which she won. It was finally agreed that they could enter America provided they married within five days of the event.

Marie continued her Canadian tour. The people there were kindly and they listened tolerantly to her opinions of the States; pretty strong ones. The affair had made her deeply bitter, something she had never been before. It made her resent criticisms of herself or her art which had amused her in the past. In Vancouver an editor of a local paper wrote hard things about her. She let action answer his article. She called on him and thrashed him. He had Ellis Island to thank for that.

Marie was allowed to play in America, provided she and Dillon were married, and provided that they left by the end of March 1914. They crossed the border into Oregon and at Portland in the British Consulate, Marie Lloyd became Mrs. Bernard Dillon on February 22nd, 1914.

It was a matter of conjecture in New York whether she would succeed or not. New Yorkers loved Alice, her sister, and some of them had seen Marie, but her success was problematical. Londoners and the British in the city rallied; Ellis Island had angered them. The *Olympic* was in port again and the crew went to the opening night and yelled 'Good Old Marie. London's with you'. She succeeded. One or two of the critics carped and recalled her age, scandals, and tried to disparage. But her genius—so true, so complete, so wholly genuine—conquered New York and everywhere else that she went. The audience rejoiced in the woman and bathed in her radiance. Maybe Ellis Island had helped, but the American audience acclaimed the woman it wanted to deport.

But Marie vowed she would never return to the U.S.A. She wanted to come home, and at home Alec Hurley lay dying of pneumonia. In his thoughts was the woman he loved and who had loved him. Their life was over but his love remained and flickered up again. 'Tell Marie,' he told a friend, 'that I love her as much now as the first day I saw her. She knows how much that is. Tell her that—because you'll see her again—but I shall not.' . . . So Alec died, with Marie in his heart and his thoughts.

XI

TOWARDS THE END

WHEN the American tour ended and New York reporters came to see Marie take ship for England, she frankly told them that she never would return to the United States.

When they asked her the usual question: 'What do you think of America'; she pointed to the Statue of Liberty.

'I think your sense of humour is grand,' she drily commented.

It was 1914 and the world was about to change and her world was changing too; already she had found that her marriage with Dillon had been a tragic mistake.

The charming Irishman, superb horseman, singer of love songs, was not a good husband. His true colours became apparent. He was cruel, violent; the real 'colours' were different from the gay silks he had worn when racing. He was no longer a jockey; the turf authorities and he held different opinions on the question of riding. But he was Marie Lloyd's husband and that, he decided, was a pretty good life. He had used his whip on horses and now used it, or his fists, upon his wife. He drank; brawled and was altogether impossible. Yet his spell over her seemed complete. She would not get rid of him.

Like many of the Music Hall folk, Marie lunched

at the Queen's Hotel in Leicester Square where 'Bunnie' worked. 'Bunnie' was one of the real bar-maids of those days, a woman of the world, possessed of the judgment and worldly wisdom of Solomon and with far more common sense. She saw Marie one day stylishly dressed as usual but wearing a thick veil and she sensed the reason for the disguise—bruises.

'Why don't you get rid of him, Marie?' she asked. 'Well, my dear,' answered Marie, 'you see, he's my husband, and I love him.'

She said that to everyone who pleaded with her to take a sensible course. Like all of her calling, she was superstitious and she held on desperately to the idea that the third time, in due course, would be lucky. But it was not.

War broke out and life changed. Marie did not embark on a series of topical songs as did most Music Hall performers. The 'act' was established. Her only concession to this new awe-inspiring war was a characteristic song, *I do like yer, cocky, now you've got yer khaki on*. She did far more good by working the Halls, packed with men in training, men en route to the Front, or men back home from trench warfare for a few brief hours, by just being Marie Lloyd and making them forget the horrible world outside. She expressed to them the warm feminine charm and camaraderie for which they were famished. She brought them home to the spirit of this land, which makes its best jokes when in its direst straits. She sang her old popular songs—she sang *I shall never forget the days when I was young*, and the soldiers loved her and howled the chorus. For already one's childhood seemed so far away; age came quickly in the First World War; but Marie seemed so young, so gay and so completely changeless that it was quite wonderful to see her. Once on the stage her own worries fell from her. Here she was 'Queen' and the servant of her subjects, the public. She felt that always, right up to the end. Many players profess that feeling whilst secretly they cherish a pretty strong contempt for those they serve. Marie was sincere. It possessed her on the boards.

Back in the dressing-room, her cares and sorrows would assail her and the years would show on the face which had once been bright. But for her audience it was her duty to drive cares away. She was a dutiful artiste. She was in the last phase of her songs by now but they still loved the old ones and clamoured for *A Little of What You Fancy—Everything in the Garden's Lovely* and her song about *Men and Women*, where she gave her ideas as to what women thought of men. The present generation has forgotten that song, but it was by far one of her best. And at this time she was ready for the two immortal songs which—coming as they did at the end of her career, placed a crown upon it which will always be remembered—showed her at her best, as singer, actress and comedienne, as Marie Lloyd. They were *One of the Ruins that Cromwell Knocked About a Bit* and *The Old Cock Linnet*, the real title of which is *Don't Dilly-Dally on the Way*. Those weren't only songs, but great performances. Magic and melody

were in them; and she gave them the rich flavours of
superb character performances.

There she was, the good, homely lady—*not* above
a little bit of fun, but basically respectable—doing no
worse than her neighbours, anyway. This typical
woman of her class suddenly developed an interest in
history on account of a ruined abbey she saw on a
short visit to the country. She learned that a man
named Cromwell had been responsible for its ruinous
condition and whilst musing on this, a gentleman
spoke to her and asked for information concerning the
ancient monument. It was a good opening gambit.
She was glad of company and glad to be of use to
him. 'It's one of the ruins that Cromwell knocked
about a bit,' she said, and explained that judging
from its appearance, there had been lots of 'doings'
in the old days. Small wonder that the poor old abbey
had suffered. She gave the gentleman all the information she possessed. A stroll in the woods resulted and
poor Marie, at the end, discovered that she had been
'buzzed'; in other words the nicely spoken gentleman
had relieved her of her purse. The awakening was
sad, but maybe her own fault, for prior to the stroll
they had visited a pub opposite the abbey and
lingered there, partaking of refreshment. The name
of the pub was the Cromwell Arms. With the vision
of the ruin wrought by Cromwell, Marie had become
indignant. She wanted to know where Cromwell
could be found, so that she might give him a piece of
her mind, there seems reason to believe that she
thought he was the landlord. Sad to say, she was
ejected, and she told her audience *Outside the*

Cromwell Arms, last Saturday night, I was one of the ruins that Cromwell knocked abaht a bit. It was a grand song, a grand tune. She was magnificent.

So, too, was the lady with the cock linnet. Again Marie was the same type of woman, so many of whom were in the audiences which loved her. She and her old man had to move away from their home, and the day was trying. The furniture removers were inefficient and broke many of her treasures, which she deplored and finally when they had taken all the furniture from the house the van was full and there was room only for her husband. It was essential, according to him, that he should go with the stuff, to show the men where to put it at the new home. So Marie had to walk; consigned to her care was the family pet, the old cock linnet in its cage.

Her husband told her the route she must follow. It was quite simple, he said, all she had to do was to follow the van and not to hang about or dilly-dally. And so, off went the van with all her possessions. She, according to orders, was to follow on with the old cock linnet. She did her best. She tried. But she was tired, she had had an awful day and so she dillied and dallied; the dalliance took place in conveniently situated pubs and included 'half-quarterns' to keep up her spirits. The inevitable happened. She did not know which way to go, for the van was out of sight. Lost and forlorn with only the old cock linnet for company, she felt so faint and hungry that she informed the creature that if she didn't land home pretty soon, she would eat his birdseed. Hopeless and grim life was a tragedy; she did not know where to

turn for help for, she told us, she couldn't trust the
Specials like the old time coppers and she couldn't
find her way home.

The performance was a masterpiece. It was the
very zenith of the art of Music Hall and the heart of
the art of acting. Those who saw and heard Marie in
those songs cherish the memory. Those who had the
misfortune not to do so, missed a chance which will
never come again. There was beneath the riotous
comedy, a note of sadness, a tragedy in a minor key.
The lady who was interested in ruins had a rude
awakening. That gentleman in whom she had confided
'buzzed' her of her purse; and the straight road for
the other had become hard and stony and she was,
indeed, completely lost because she had used it as
the primrose path of dalliance. Life was sad. Life
was hollow.

Her public goodwill never was greater. Her private
happiness was almost non-existent. Dillon made life
a purgatory for her. He beat her and disgraced her,
he upset the peace of the home she loved so much.
Constantly in trouble, he had joined the forces during
the war and deserted; he became an absentee and
was publicly prosecuted. He was always being
arrested and fined for fighting and assaults. And
always her name cropped up. In every way, he made
her life sorrowful. Her family, who loved her, tried
to protect her, but Bernard Dillon, enraged and in his
cups was a devil incarnate. Nothing and nobody were
sacred to him, age did not matter nor did sex. If
there was a bashing to be done, in his estimation, he
did it. What poor Marie suffered can be imagined.

It would be easy to say that she deserved it; she had chosen the way herself; each time she married disaster followed; she ought to have known better. It would be less easy to justify such censure. It must be remembered that Marie was not the normal woman of everyday life; she was a Bohemian, a nomad. She had a good father and mother; she was a good daughter to them; she was a good sister to her brothers and sisters and a wonderful friend to multitudes. But within her was that madness which is part of a true performer; that touch of insanity, that disregard of normal ways which always goes with the artiste. There are degrees of it, of course, but so often the greater the genius, the greater the artistic unrest of mind, the greater the disregard for the common rules of life. Marie was a rebel and she had carved out her own career. Life had begun very early and great success had come when she was only a child. When in her teens she had married the wrong man and she had been introduced to him by a young man who at that time considered himself engaged to her and who lamented afterwards in the words of the famous Music Hall song, *Never introduce your Donah to a Pal*. She had not looked below the surface then; she never did at any time of her life. That was Marie's greatest failing. She took things at face value and she, herself, assessed that value. If a thing pleased her, she did not care what anyone else said. She would give advice—but she would never take it. And she was a public idol who was universally beloved. It often follows that the admiration of many prevents the love of the one.

Marie saw her first marital mistake. When again she had thought she had discovered the right man in a gay Cockney, fundamentally she had, for she loved Alec Hurley and he loved her. That their marriage failed was due to mutual faults, professional jealousy and weakness of mind on his part, vanity, recklessness and obstinacy on hers. The third, a major disaster, came when the mature Marie, who considered herself a wise woman of the world, had been dazzled by glitter which might have attracted a youngster, but through which she ought to have seen. But she made her mistake and bitterly she paid in happiness, health and money. As proudly as she could she bore it all and tried to hide her sorrow from the world. But no one could disguise a violent gangster like Bernard Dillon nor disguise his works.

Marie was a fine specimen of feminine illogicality. Attack a person and she became his violent champion. One had only to say somebody was a villain to make her sure he was a hero. Always the upholder of the under-dog, she never realized that many of these animals were mongrel curs and unworthy of a thought from her.

She tried travel to ease her pain and went to South Africa again. When she was very much younger she had been there and scored a triumph. Again she did so. People who remembered seeing her perform were amazed to find so little change in her; it seemed that age could not wither her nor custom stale her infinite variety. On the stage she looked as young; in performance she was more brilliant than ever. But away from the public she was a sad and lonely woman, so lonely that she feared to be alone for one moment. She was frightened of her thoughts and afraid to go to bed; she must have company, lights, parties and all that went with them. Maybe there was more appeal to those tonics which are always ready to hand, the sips of brandy when one felt 'down' as one always did, the bottles of champagne which could, for the moment, fill life with their own sparkle and tint it to their golden hue—but leave life flat and bitter when the fizz evaporated. She began to know fear; the life she had loved became a menace to her. Outwardly in company, or on the stage, there was the changeless Marie Lloyd, but out of the glitter, when there was no pretence but only the reality around her, she was becoming an old hag-ridden woman. Sometimes, even the radiance seemed to be in eclipse. She still gave royally; but giving did not give her the same zest. She had the ceaseless drain of a bad man upon her, a spot of rust which seemed to be eating into her brilliance and corroding it away.

To put life behind her, to keep down remorse and regrets she plunged into work; she drove herself and worked far too hard. Her earnings were enormous; but what good were they to her? She never could keep money; the only use she had for it was to spend or give it away. The beloved home was not a place of rest; it had become a perpetual battlefield. She had begun at £100 a week when she was seventeen; now she was earning weekly over six times that amount. Already around her, the Empires, the Hippodromes and the Palaces and Coliseums up and down the country were losing grip before the onslaught of the films. True Music Hall was dying, largely because its individualists had sunk their individuality, the very backbone and marrow of Variety, into team work called Revue. Times were hard; business was bad; but whenever the name of Marie Lloyd was billed, the Halls were packed. She restored smiles to managerial faces and brightness to the masses of a war-weary people beginning to feel the pinch of Peace. It seemed indeed as if Marie were herself Music Hall; and in truth that is what she was. It explains so much of her when that is realized.

She worked far too hard. She was no longer young and her strength was going. She had no relief, no real peace, no chance of relaxation. She knew no other life save that which she had always led; she had no intellectual or cultural relaxations to ease the strain. In her twilight of trouble, she turned to work and giving. Each night she had an injection, not from the hypodermic of a doctor, but from the applause of the multitude. It kept her going, but wore off too soon. Trouble lurked in every corner, in every hour, in every telephone call, in every knock on the door. She lived in a state of constant apprehension. But she never lost her kindliness, gentleness towards the sorrow and stress of others. Much of the buoyancy and the brilliance which had been hers was there only when she faced an audience; despite the unending strain she never lost her looks and she always retained her prettiness. No doubt she regarded that as a trust for her public. But so much else had gone and the ailments, common to many people who are nearing middle age crept on. Rheumatism gave her pangs at times and she, who had always liked good food, and who knew how to cook it, began to lose interest in what she ate. Out of those blue eyes, which once gave forth a sparkle of gaiety, there peeped now only sadness.

She began to find it hard to memorize and she had once learned each new song in a few minutes. Shading and building them up had been a joy to her; now she found it weary labour. But never once did she dry-up before an audience and she never once let it see the sorrow which was eating her. To the public she was always 'Our Marie'. A tired, worn out woman she would stand at the side, waiting for the moment to enter, sagging a little, all the fun and chaff with the staff gone; but the moment the cue came—the moment the band reached the right bar—then Marie Lloyd was herself again and the house rose at her. She had medical treatment, but there was no real complaint; there was nothing tangible that medicine or treatment could cure. She was going downhill of her own volition. The complaint was incurable, some might call it heartbreak, perhaps a less sentimental diagnosis is disillusionment. She tried to fight it with work but it was too deep rooted and could not be subdued.

At Edmonton, Marie became very ill indeed. They called her own doctor. He told her not to play and might well have spoken to a granite tower. The audience was there; she was there and on she went. There were pitiful scenes afterwards in her dressing-room, but Marie had kept faith. After the second house she was taken home to bed. On time she arrived at the theatre next evening, although she collapsed into a chair in her dressing-room. She was early and she said she wanted to rest before going on. But she got worse and worse. The doctor arrived and he forbade her to appear. But from her room she could hear the people going in, crowds and crowds of them because she was appearing; she heard them mention her name; they had come because of her. Marie would not break faith. Everyone did their best to prevent her from playing; it would have been obvious to a blind man that she was dangerously ill and not fit to stand, let alone go on the stage and make the exhausting effort that entertaining an audience entailed, especially in Marie's way. But they could not dissuade her. They helped her and she struggled into her costume and put on her make-up. She was ready in spirit if not in body. Her number went up. At the very last minute her friends implored her. 'They will understand, Marie.' 'I understand what I am doing, too,' she answered. 'The boys and girls out there have come to see me. Hark at them now, they are applauding already, bless their hearts. They are calling my name, can't you hear? Of course, I'm going on so long as I can walk. I'll be all right when I'm "on". I'll get through.' She made her entrance.

She got that thunderous roar of applause, those loud handclaps, those piercing whistles, those shouts of 'Good old Marie'; and as usual she responded. Shaking off the support of the manager and her dressers, she went on and that smile sparkled out, those eyes shone, that wink went over and those

hands spoke for themselves. Not for one moment did
the audience suspect. She finished her number and
she worked her full complement. When it came to
her last song, somehow she made the change. And
then, to the audience's joy, she sang *I'm One of the
Ruins that Cromwell Knocked abaht a Bit*. They
whistled it; they sang it with her. Maybe a keener
eye or two noted that the staggers which formed part
of the song were a little more marked, a little more
prolonged; that there was a glaze in the eyes, a slight
slurring in the usually perfect diction; that the reeling
of the intoxicated woman was a bit more realistic.
But the applause was more violent than usual, too.

What was passing in Marie's mind nobody will
ever know. What she did must have been done auto-
matically; it was none the less perfect. She must
have been aware that she was not alone on that
stage and that for once she, the individualist, had a
partner and was part of a double turn. The name of
the partner was Death. But she cheated him of a
triumph; she held on to the end, and at the end she
got the biggest laugh yet. For, seemingly overcome by
the liquor from the Cromwell Arms, she did something she had never done before in that song—as the
last words came from her lips, *I was one of the ruins
that Cromwell knocked abaht a bit*—she fell. Before
them she crumbled into ruins and lay upon the stage.
The curtain fell. The 'boys and girls' stamped; they
shouted, they applauded. She took no curtain to
thank them. The next number went up and the show
went on.

Marie was carried to the chair in her room and

later she was taken home. She regained consciousness and spoke of the second house, still saying that all she wanted was 'a little rest'. How true that was, poor soul. She had had so little rest. Despite her desire to play on, they took her home to bed and never again did her number go up in the frame. Never again did Marie hear that welcome roar, never again those words of 'Good Old Marie'. She had answered her last call.

XII

IMMORTALITY

THE news of Marie's death on October 7th, 1922, shook the nation. Even those who disapproved of her, and her way of life and who had never seen her, felt a shock. It seemed as if something that was part of the British Way of Life had passed. But to hundreds of thousands, nay to millions, there came a feeling of deep personal loss, a grief as deep and natural as if somebody who was really near to them and the best beloved had passed away. They could not quite believe it. She had always seemed so young (and indeed she was only fifty-two), so gay, so lively, so full of vitality that it seemed death could never touch her and maybe they were right.

They mourned her and took the only possible way of showing their genuine grief. Men who have served their country, soldiers, sailors, statesmen, and the like, have funerals which are decked with official pomp and ceremony. They wind their way on their last journey between crowds who stand and watch with respect and veneration. They go to the sacred mausoleums, Westminster Abbey or St. Paul's Cathedral, where their last resting-places will be monuments. There is not much real grief amongst the crowds who watch; regrets maybe, admiration maybe, but not much personal feeling or love. But from time to time, there arises a public figure who gains such reverent affection in a private capacity, not through professional service to the State, but through professional service to the people. Then can be seen a tribute superbly poignant, a whole people mourning a beloved friend.

This does not happen often; the people who arouse such feelings are few. Despite the large number of stars of the entertainment world, only a few get the public tribute of grateful love and affection. The public tribute was given to Marie Lloyd. She had been excluded from a Royal Command Performance, but went to her last rest in a manner Royalty might have envied.

It was, perhaps, the most amazing funeral ever seen, in its spontaneous outburst of deep and personal feeling. For there was public mourning without any official order, public mourning by public demand, just as she had threatened in return for the slight over the Royal performance. There have been few tributes like it. The public paid such tributes to the passing of Fred Leslie, William Terriss, Dan Leno, Tommy Handley, and Ivor Novello; shops were closed en route, and deep serried ranks stood in silence as each passed before the audience for the last time.

The funeral of Irving was different. He was buried in Westminster Abbey, and his ashes were carried there the night before, through streets lined by people. The abbey itself was thronged for the service. There was respect and grief at the going of a great man. With Ivor Novello it was his loyalty to his public and his gift of giving them colour, romance,

and melody—of gilding their grey days—that won
their love and that last amazing exit. With Marie
Lloyd it was just herself.

She knew nothing of films or radio. She was just
a woman who had won their hearts, with her gift of
happiness to them, with the sunshine which had
brought with her radiance. She was never more 'Our
Marie' than on the day when she went amongst the
public for the last time.

They loved her, and they said it with flowers, with
tears, with their personal presence as far as they
could. Her house could not contain the wreaths
which flowed in like the flooding of an ocean, from
all ranks and stations, of all shapes and sizes, from
great creations of the florist's art down to penny
bunches of violets. They overflowed into the house
in which she had lived previously—Oak Dene, which
was vacant at the time. They came from all sorts and
conditions of people. Every star of the Music Hall
sent one, and there were tributes from a Piccadilly
flower-seller, the taxi-drivers of a nearby garage, and
one from the Costermongers' Union of Farringdon
Road. Some were anonymous; there was a large
white cushion of flowers with the word 'Till' inscribed
on it in violets and a cluster of pink carnations in the
corner. Another bore the legend 'With everlasting
regret and loving remembrance from a life-long
friend'. A near relation sent a model arm-chair in
flowers, a replica of the chair she liked the most.
From seven sisters came seven hearts of flowers, each
in a different colour. There was a horseshoe of white
chrysanthemums with whip, spurs, and cap attached

—the cap in blue flowers—with the inscription, 'From her Jockey Pals'. There was a bird-cage of flowers, symbolic of her last great song. The door stood open; the bird and the singer were gone.

An enormous model of a stage, with the word 'Finis' on the proscenium arch on each side where her 'number' would have been, and on the front of the stage a great bunch of roses, as if for her last tribute. It came from Walter Bentley, her last agent, and his wife. There was a cushion of flowers from Bombardier Billy Wells, the heavyweight boxing champion. Perhaps the most unusual was a model of the sort of box that dressmakers send home their completed frocks in. It bore on it, 'From Arthur, with heartfelt sympathy and deepest regrets. My last design, the dress-box but no dress. To my dear Marie.' It was from Jefferson Arthur Leake, who designed and made her dresses in her later years. From Music Halls and clubs came the deluge of flowers; from the National Sporting Club, the Eccentric Club, the Ladies' Theatrical Guild, the Variety Artistes' Federation, from members of the legitimate branch of the 'profession', from Julia Neilson and Fred Terry, from Connie Ediss of the Gaiety—who had started on the Halls—from the Camberwell Palace, from the Ring at Blackfriars, from Major Arnold Wilson (the fight promoter), Lady Brickwood, Sir Walter and Lady de Frece (Vesta Tilley), Sir Oswald Stoll, Charles Gulliver; from every star and almost every performer of any note, came flowers. They even filled her garden with a greater mass of bloom than had ever grown there. And when the procession started—twelve motor-cars packed with flowers went ahead of the hearse. On the front of her hearse was that long black stick she used when singing her Directoire song—a 'prop' of which she was fond. With her in the hearse were the flowers of her dearest: her mother and father, her daughter, and her sisters, Alice, Daisy and rest of the family. And one also from her husband. The wreath from her parents lay at her feet.

Cars carrying friends and mourners followed her. The roof of each was packed with wreaths, and the inside with famous names. Immediately behind the hearse came her own car, with the chauffeur who had driven her for fifteen years at the wheel. Its blinds were drawn down, but through a gap one could see the rug thrown back over the seat, as she must have left it.

The people—the men and women who were her public and her dear friends—followed the procession. They had come from all quarters, in all sorts of ways: some in smart cars, some in omnibuses, some on bicycles, some on costers' barrows, and thousands on foot. It was a short distance from where she lived to St. Luke's Church, Hampstead, where the service was held, and thence to Fortune Green Cemetery. The route was lined on each side until there was no more room. The church was packed until the doors had to be closed.

The people in the church waited for hours, as did those by the roadside. And then, shortly before the cortège arrived, an old man in humble clothes knocked on the church door until they opened it. He begged admittance, and they told him there was no room, and prepared to shut the door again. Tears ran down his cheeks. 'I'm turned seventy,' he said. 'I sang in the same halls as she did thirty years ago. Marie was always good and kind to me. I've walked such a long way to say good-bye to her. Please let me in.' He was so simple, so sincere, and so obviously genuine that he was squeezed in to stand at the back. There were thousands like him in the ever-growing crowd outside. Mounted police had to control the multitude, and in it all ranks rubbed shoulders, gentle and simple, rich and poor, come to pay a last respect and say good-bye to one they loved and to whom they owed much happiness.

Many more had gone straight to the cemetery. Their wait was made longer by the crowds which covered the roadway and held up the procession for over half an hour after the expected time of arrival. They stood talking amongst themselves, telling stories about her, recalling half-forgotten things and songs and sayings, until at long last the hearse came into sight. A deep silence fell. Every hat came off every man's head, and only the weeping and sobbing women broke the hush. Slowly Marie passed between her subjects to where she was to be laid in her grave. There were over five thousand people round her. The committal service was read and a silence of prayer followed.

When the mourners-in-chief had gone, Marie's public showed their homage. Many of the people kissed their flowers before dropping them into the grave, sure that their caress would reach her. For hours and hours they filed by, slowly, silent but for sobs, all sadly proud to take farewell of the woman who had given them brightness—and adding what brightness they could by their flowers. Fifty thousand people paid their tribute of love and gratitude to what lay within that grave—and went away, sad-eyed—to face a world which had lost some of its sunshine—to remember a friend who had given them so much help in her brief span of life.

It was dusk before that final audience of hers had passed by to wish her well and store their memory with one last thought of her. A day without parallel in the history of the entertainment world was over, and it seemed that, with the night and the darkness, the glare and glitter of the Music Halls would never be so bright again. The twilight of Variety had settled down. And one last glimpse of that day which, I believe, has not yet been recorded.

A man sitting in one of the cars that followed Marie on her last journey saw something which has always lived in his memory as being as typical of her as of Music Hall. The carriage had turned into the cemetery and was moving at a slow walking-pace. It was absolutely packed with at least four more people than it could reasonably hold. In the corner sat a performer, quite well known, but not a star; he had never reached greater eminence than middle of the bill in the smaller halls. But he was a friend of Marie's and was overcome with emotion. He had been weeping openly, and now sat with his face turned to the window, staring out at the graves which lay on either side. Suddenly the carriage halted, and he peered forward. There was a gap in the crowd, and he saw something. He pulled down the window, leant out and reached upwards to where the wreaths lay piled on top. Seizing one, just as the carriage started again, he flung it on to a grave. The man sat back with a look of subdued satisfaction. Everyone stared at him, but nobody asked the question which was on every lip. Gazing round at his fellow-travellers, he explained, with a jerk of his thumb in the direction in which he had thrown the wreath. 'Lottie Collins,' he said. 'She lies there. Marie wouldn't have minded.'

Everyone nodded their heads in approval. For he had expressed Marie Lloyd in those four words. Marie would not have minded sharing her flowers with Lottie Collins; indeed, it was just the sort of thing she would have done herself.

THE AUTHOR EXPLAINS

IT is doubtful if anyone ever reads a preface or a foreword. But, if they have enjoyed a book, they may be trapped into reading an epilogue. So on the off-chance that I may have been lucky enough to have found somebody who has read this book through, I append these last few words. I have made no attempt to write an authoritative, chronological, and exhaustively detailed story of the life of Marie Lloyd. It is very doubtful if such a book could be written in a satisfactory manner. The people of Music Hall did not leave the pile of documentation that their brethren of the Theatre accumulate. They had remarkably little publicity at any time and they did not need it.

There were a very great number of them at one time, but in another fifty years, not more than a score, one prophesies, will be remembered. Their songs, yes; but people will forget who sang them. The few names that will be immortal? Who will they be? George Robey, for certain; Harry Lauder, just as certain; Vesta Tilley; Eugene Stratton, perhaps (although even today people think that the singer of *The Lily of Laguna* is G. H. Elliott); Harry Tate, yes—he is immortal, and probably there always will be a Harry Tate moustache; Little Tich, maybe because of his physical peculiarity and the expression 'tichy', meaning small; Chirgwin may linger because of his white eye; Gracie Fields; the Crazy Gang (one has a pious hope); Albert Chevalier; Fred Karno (who was a supreme producer whose name became a comic trademark); and Dan Leno and Marie Lloyd.

To Marie there is a legend attached; the legend that she was the naughtiest woman in England, the pivot of smoking-room stories, of suggestiveness or, as the more vulgar put it—of dirt. That reputation she does not deserve. As time has gone on, there has grown a belief that she was a woman of loose behaviour, whose own character was the same as the implications of her songs. That is false, and if he has read this book, it is hoped that the reader is convinced that Marie was inherently good. If it comes to a question of plain Christianity, of doing unto others as you would be done by, she was an extremely good example of what Christians should be. In her make-up she was something of the saint—note the qualification, 'in her own way'. I would be the last to imagine or to think of her as a saint. But few people did as much good as she in her passage through this world. In all her life she never was guilty of an ungenerous action; she never harmed a soul. Her life was not saintly; she was a woman of her world. She knew that world and had a very clear knowledge of the difference between right and wrong. She had many, many faults, but malice, envy, greed, double-dealing, deceit, sharp practice, and falsehood had no place in the list.

From time to time men and women write of her disparagingly and give false impressions. None of them is old enough to have seen, let alone known her. They form their conclusions on the legend. When this occurs, apart from her own family, or those who survive, Marie has two champions: my humble self and my friend Naomi (Mickie) Jacob, the eminent novelist. We take up the battle and we always win. Both of us, not only saw her, but knew her. Mickie Jacob knew her more intimately than I, and she wrote a fully detailed life, a most valuable book, to which I wish to render acknowledgments in the compilation of this one.

I knew her, too, and I have few gifts; but one of these is an understanding of the profession to which Marie and I belonged, and at one time Mickie Jacob adorned. It is still my profession. The gods have not given me much, but they have bestowed on me a little talent for observation and judgment of what I see and a memory that never lets go of anything seen or of something once read or heard. I have used those small powers to the best of my ability here.

Let us try to give a fair assessment of Marie Lloyd in as few words as possible, just to fill in omissions and to amplify things which may not have been made clear.

She was basically a woman of her own class; from that standard she never departed. She did not want to. She had no refinement, in the Kensingtonian or Bloomsbury meaning of the word. She was of the people; to them she remained true. Is it surprising, therefore, that they remained true to her? That is why they called her 'Our Marie'.

Her manner of singing her songs had its basis on that. She knew what were the people's views on life. She knew the saloon bars and the bar parlours, the racecourses, the parties, the language of the shops, the barrows and the bookies; and what the women said to each other over the garden wall or over the cups of tea in the kitchen. And she mirrored all those things. That was her job and she did it superbly. Nobody has done it better. In real life, she was not careful in her speech; she did not mince matters; she called a spade a spade, a man or woman whom she happened to dislike or who angered her—names which in both cases began with a 'B'. But her songs were never inherently 'dirty'. Once they brought her one which horrified her: 'But this is about a lavatory,' she said—and threw it out. It offended her. It struck her as indecent. What, one wonders, would she have thought today?

Songs which would have meant nothing when sung by other 'serio-comics', became in her hands things of delight. Consider *Then You Wink the Other Eye*. Here is the chorus:

> *Say, boys, now is it quite the thing?*
> *Say, should we let you have your fling?*
> *Oh, when you've got us on a string,*
> *Then you wink the other eye.*

She made that song. I have often thought of her songs in connection with the ditty which made so much fame for my dear friend Ellaline Terriss.

> *Just a little bit of string,*
> *Such a tiny little thing;*
> *Shall she tell us what the string may be?*
> *Make him put his slippers on*
> *And be sure his boots have gone,*
> *And you've got him on a string, you see.*

What would Marie Lloyd have made of that? One can guess. Or that other famous song at the Gaiety, *The Boy Guessed Right*.

> *And the boy guessed right the very first time,*
> *The very first time, the very first time,*
> *He knew by the sound it was not a pussy cat,*
> *It's funny how he came to think of that.*

Again, imagine Marie—what that face, that wink, those wonderfully expressive hands would have made of the arrival of the new baby. As sung by Ella with her sweet simplicity, her calm beauty, her little turned-up nose, and her wild-rose freshness, they were entrancing songs. As sung by Marie Lloyd, they would have been riots of another kind. For without saying a word, she would have supplied all the background, all the amorousness and preparation beforehand—the lot—as they say today. But by mere suggestion. In that sense she was suggestive. With Ellaline Terriss—a genius of another kind—it was innocent sweetness; with Marie Lloyd it would have been full-blooded humanity. Different methods, both superb. It may shock some to realize that one of the greatest geniuses our stage ever produced had as the bedrock of her talent, sauciness. It is the word which best describes her and her art. Sir Louis Fergusson sums it up: 'But a woman of genius Marie Lloyd surely was, and of sauciness her genius consisted, however incongruous it seems. There should never be any suspicion of patronizing the memory of Marie Lloyd, of trying to apologize for her or explain her away. There she stood, facing up indomitably to her

Music Hall audience—inexplicable her genius may be, impossible to recapture, impossible to analyse.' Hazlitt would have hailed it as 'the complete thing'. How right Hazlitt would have been and how right Sir Louis is, in his perfect summing-up of Marie Lloyd.

It is becoming more and more prevalent for writers of history to indulge in what is called 'debunking'. I submit that this is not true history, any more than the type of criticism which merely denounces is true criticism. As these lines are being written, King Edward VII is being debunked. I lived in his reign and I know how much good he did, how much he was part and parcel of the life around him and how much he was able to understand it. People not alive then have no conception to what extent the failings they point out contributed to his greatness. He was a monarch who was loved; he was popular and, being popular, he was near his people and able to understand them. He himself never made claims to greatness, but he was one of the ablest statesmen of his time and understood what was good for his country and his people. He gave them pleasure and joy because he mixed with them and participated in their pastimes; he believed in the English, despite the guttural accent. He gave his name to an epoch.

The great thing about Marie Lloyd also was her understanding. She would have been the same today. She was not a statuesque, classic beauty; she was adorably pretty and full of vivid attraction. Even the physical fault of her slightly protruding teeth suited her and set off her prettiness. It was one of those imperfections which throw up the perfections—it was part of the light and shade. She sparkled and she wore her clothes to perfection. Her figure was a woman's figure in good proportion, without that. exaggeration on certain feminine features which has such a vogue today. She had a bust, of course, but a bust which fitted her. She was essentially feminine, loved clothes and understood them. I should imagine that she loved that Directoire dress of hers best of all—it certainly was, in the slang of the day, a 'stunner'. It was not vulgar or *outré*. The slashed skirt revealed as shapely a leg and ankle as any vaunted film star today can show. I am sure she loved it, and that was why the stick which accompanied it went with her to the grave.

Despite the fact that she was divorced twice, there was no vice in her. If she lived with a man before she married him—well, she married him in the end and whilst they were together, wed or unwed, she kept to him. She did not share her favours as she shared her money. That she lavished, broadcast; her favours were reserved for the man she loved. She was as honest as she was clean, and she was a spotless person. She was not a moral woman in the conventional idea of her time; she lived in Bohemia. But her morals would compare favourably with many Hollywood stars of both sexes. There were no casual love affairs. If she was not moral, she was certainly not amoral.

Yet her life was a sad one. She gave undiluted pleasure to millions and brought the gleam of happiness into grey, unhappy lives. She never found happiness herself. She wanted the love and companionship of a husband to whom she could be Chevalier's 'My Old Dutch'. She never got it. Some of the faults were hers. But it was never sexual unfaithfulness which brought the disasters. It was mostly that genius of hers which was as unlucky to her as it was lucky to others and which she could not help, which was the axe causing the cleavage. Her third venture, from which she hoped so much, was her greatest mistake. She had little excuse for it—she was old enough to see things as they were and as they would be. She listened to nobody. She wanted love and she wanted to be loved. The aspiration dazzled her. The result was tragedy that clouded what remained of her life and brought reflected degradation on her.

Of Marie's generosity, no more need be said. It has been mentioned time and again. It was prodigal, foolish, and far too lavish; it was Marie Lloyd. It was all the joy she got out of life, save the success she achieved and that wonderful pride which comes from the superb audience control and the acclaim of the multitude.

The little woman from Hoxton is immortal and likely to endure in memory as long as the English tongue survives. Today she is a legend, a tradition, and the British cling to such things. When they cease to do so, they will cease to be British. May that day be far away.

People will still talk of Marie. She walks the boards of tradition as confidently as she walked the boards of the Music Halls. Those who arouse love and affection have somehow the power of sending a reflection of it down the ages. The memory of Nell Gwyn lives. Marie Lloyd's name will endure. Her radiance will shine down the centuries.

Ur.   ®

Ur   ®

Ur

®

Milton Keynes UK
Ingram Content Group UK Ltd.
UKHW022344220124
436511UK00005B/219